A Sourcebook of
Classical Hindu Thought

Contemporary Researches in Hindu Philosophy & Religion

(ISSN 0971-9628)

1. Idealistic Thought in Indian Philosophy; by Shuchita C. Divatia (ISBN 978-81-246-0021-4)
2. Karma and Reincarnation: The Vedāntic Perspective; by Muni Narayana Prasad (ISBN 978-81-246-0022-1)
3. Stonemill and Bhakti: From the Devotion of Peasant Women to the Philosophy of Swamies; by Guy Poitevin and Hema Rairkar (ISBN 978-81-246-0059-7)
4. Śaivism: Some Glimpses; by G.V. Tagare (ISBN 978-81-246-0076-4)
5. Advaita: A Conceptual Analysis; by A. Ramamurty (ISBN 978-81-246-0067-2)
6. Mind-Body Dualism: A Philosophic Investigation; by Alpana Chakraborty (ISBN 978-81-246-0071-9)
7. Hinduism and Scientific Quest; by T.R.R. Iyengar (ISBN 978-81-246-0077-1)
8. Indra and Other Vedic Deities — A Euhemeristic Study; by Uma Chakravarty (ISBN 978-81-246-0080-1)
9. Brahma-Vāda: Doctrine of Śrī Vallabhācārya; by G.V. Tagare (ISBN 978-81-246-0112-9)
10. The Science of Enlightenment: Enlightenment, Liberation and God — A Scientific Explanation; by Nitin Trasi (ISBN 978-81-246-0130-3)
11. Retrieving Sāṁkhya History: An Ascent from Dawn to Meridian; by Lallanji Gopal (ISBN 978-81-246-0143-3)
12. The Philosophical Foundations of Hinduism; by A. Ramamurty (ISBN 978-81-246-0163-1)
13. The Eternal Hinduism; by Baidyanath Saraswati (ISBN 978-81-246-0249-2)
14. Vedanta and its Philosophical Development; by A. Ramamurty (ISBN 978-81-246-0347-5)
15. Sāṁkhya-Yoga Epistomology; by Mukta Biswas (ISBN 978-81-246-0371-0)

Contemporary Researches in Hindu Philosophy & Religion, no. 16

A Sourcebook of Classical Hindu Thought

Arvind Sharma

PRINTWORLD
Publishers of Indian Traditions

Cataloging in Publication Data — DK
[Courtesy: D.K. Agencies (P) Ltd. <docinfo@dkagencies.com>]

Sharma, Arvind.
A sourcebook of classical Hindu thought / Arvind Sharma.
p. cm. — (Contemporary researches in Hindu philosophy & religion ; no. 16)
Includes bibliographical references.
ISBN 13: 9788124606438

1. Hindu philosophy. 2. Hinduism. I. Title. II. Series : Contemporary researches in Hindu philosophy & religion ; no. 16.

DDC 181.4 23

First published in India, 2012
ISBN 13: 978-81-246-0643-8 ISBN 10: 81-246-0643-9

Published and printed by:
D.K. Printworld (P) Ltd.
Regd. Office : *'Vedaśrī'*, F-395, Sudarshan Park
(Metro Station: Ramesh Nagar), New Delhi - 110 015
Phones : (011) 2545 3975; 2546 6019; *Fax* : (011) 2546 5926
E-mail : indology@dkprintworld.com
Web : www.dkprintworld.com

Preface

THE *Sourcebook of Classical Hindu Thought* presents material from the classical Hindu texts, and a few other sources, in accordance with a well-defined template. The purpose of this Preface is to familiarise the reader with this template.

This template presents source material pertaining to classical Hindu thought in accordance with six themes. The first theme deals with the nature of the *divine realm* in classical Hinduism, beginning with *Brahman* as the ultimate reality, and then moving on to individual deities. This material is covered in chapters 1-8. This is then followed by material pertaining to the *mundane realm* in classical Hinduism. The world in which we live, rather than the divine realm above us, constitutes the theme here and thus includes a discussion of the concepts of *jīva, saṁsāra, karma,* and *dharma*. This material is covered in chapters 9-12.

If there is a divine realm posited in classical Hinduism, and a mundane realm admitted as well, then the question arises: How are these two related to each other? This provides the third theme and is covered in chapter 13 on *māyā*.

If classical Hinduism assumes, as it does, that a person's liberation or salvation ultimately lies in establishing contact with the divine realm in such a way that the gulf between the divine realm and the mundane realm is transcended, then the question as to how this might be accomplished naturally follows. The comprehensive term for ways of making this connection between the two realms in classical Hinduism is *yoga*, through which *mokṣa* is attained. Chapters 14-17 provide source material from classical Hindu texts on these points.

It is true that the Hindu tradition talks about a divine realm, and a mundane realm, and explores the nature of their relationship and ways of crossing over. In this sense it could be said to be other-worldly. But classical Hinduism also pays close attention to the reality of a human being as a social creature. It does not look upon a human being as one merely intent on seeking liberation or salvation but accepts that human beings are social animals. This fifth theme is covered in chapters 18 to 20.

Finally the question arises: From where are all these themes emerging? From the Hindu scriptures, of course. The foundational scriptures of Hinduism, the Vedas, thus constitute the sixth and final theme of the book.

It will become obvious to the reader, as she or he goes through the book, that one theme follows another. The reader might thus wish to contemplate this template as one way of mapping the universe of classical Hinduism.

Contents

List of Abbreviations

Bh. G. Bhā.	=	*Bhagavad Gītā Bhāṣya*
Bha. Gītā	=	*Bhagavad Gītā*
Bṛ. Up. Bhā.	=	*Bṛhadāraṇyaka Upaniṣad Bhāṣya*
Bṛ. Up. or *Bṛhad.*	=	*Bṛhadāraṇyaka Upaniṣad*
BSBhā.	=	*Brahma-sūtra Bhāṣya*
Chānd.	=	*Chāndogya Upaniṣad*
Kaṭha	=	*Kaṭha Upaniṣad*
Kauśītaki	=	*Kauśītaki Brāhmaṇa Upaniṣad*
Ke. Up.	=	*Kena Upaniṣad*
Mbh.	=	*Mahābhārata*
Praśna	=	*Praśna Upaniṣad*
Taitt. Up.	=	*Taittirīya Upaniṣad*
Śvet. Up.	=	*Śvetāśvatara Upaniṣad*

1

Brahman: Ineffable

This book presents a set of readings from classical Hinduism organised around set concepts. However, the use of concepts to explain the ultimate reality and its relation to the world, and even the reality of the world, is fraught with peril. Therefore, sometimes the very exponents of the tradition have resorted to silence. Sections I and II below provide illustrations of this attitude, while section III illustrates the difficulties inherent in the use of words.

I

The following passage occurs in Śaṅkara's commentary on the *Brahma-Sūtra*. The first point to note is the non-predicability of the ultimate and the second point to note is the insistence that non-predicability does not imply non-existence. A final point to note is the fact that the difficulty is recognised as applying to not only the absolutistic but also the theistic standpoint towards the ultimate reality, before the passage ends.

> That *Brahman* is without any difference is proved by those scriptural passages also which expressly deny that it possesses any other characteristics, e.g. "Next follows the teaching by no, no" (*Bṛ. Up.* II.3.6); "It is different from the known, it is also above the unknown" (*Ke. Up.* I.4); "From whence all speech, with the mind, turns away unable to reach it" (*Taitt. Up.* II.9). Of a similar purport is that scriptural passage which relates to how Bāhva, on being questioned about *Brahman* by Vāśkalin, explained it to him by silence, "He said to him, 'Learn *Brahman*, O friend'", and became

> silent. Then, to the second and third question, he replied, "I am teaching you indeed, but you do not understand. Silent is that Self." The same teaching is conveyed by those Smṛti-texts which deny of *Brahman* all other characteristics, e.g. "I will proclaim that which is the object of knowledge, knowing which one reaches immortality; the highest *Brahman* without either beginning or end, which cannot be said either to be or not to be" (*Bha. Gītā* XIII.12). Of a similar purport is yet another Smṛti-passage, according to which the omniform Nārāyaṇa instructed Nārada, "The cause, O Nārada, of your seeing me endowed with the qualities of all beings is the *Māyā* emitted by me; do not cognise me as being such (in reality)."
>
> — Śaṅkara on *Brahma Sūtra* (III.2.17); tr. George Thibaut[1]

II

A verse is attributed to Śaṅkara, in which he bemoans having to compromise the ineffable integrity of the ultimate reality. It runs as follows:

> Forgive me, O Śiva, my three great sins. I came on a pilgrimage to Kāśī forgetting that you are omnipresent; in thinking about you I forgot that you are beyond thought; in praying to you I forgot that you are beyond words.[2]

This hymn is a useful prophylactic against falling victim to some of the stereotypes of Hinduism. One should not confuse Hinduism's images with idolatry, and the multiplicity of Gods in Hinduism with polytheism. They are just diverse runways from which the sense-laden human spirit can take off for its 'flight of the alone to the Alone'. Even village priests will

1. George Thibaut, tr., *The Vedānta-Sūtras of Bādarāyaṇa with the Commentary of Śaṅkara*, New York: Dover Publications, Inc., 1962: first published 1890 [Part I] and 1896 [Part II], Part II, p. 157.
2. S. Radhakrishnan, tr., *The Brahma-Sūtra: The Philosophy of Spiritual Life*, New York: Harper & Brothers, 1960, pp. 37-38.

frequently open their temple ceremonies with the following beloved invocation:

> O Lord, forgive the three sins that are due to my human limitations:
> Thou art everywhere, but I worship you here;
> Thou art without form, but I worship you in these forms;
> Thou needest no praise, yet I offer you these prayers and salutations.
> Lord, forgive the three sins that are due to my human limitations.[3]

III

The difficulty in communicating the nature of Reality, described in one Upaniṣad as *satyasya satyam* (the reality of the real), is also experienced not just by the scriptural texts but also by the scholiast commenting on them. The following extracts from the commentaries of Śaṅkara illustrate the point:

1. But how can the mere phrase "neither this nor that" be of any service in communicating the true nature of the principle called "the reality of the real"? It does so, we reply, by negating all varieties of apparent conditioning adjunct (*upādhi*). The Absolute is that in which there is no particularity. There is no name, no form, no action, no distinction, no universal, no attribute. It is through these determinations alone that speech proceeds, and not one of them belongs to the Absolute. So the latter cannot be taught by sentences of the pattern "This is so-and-so". In such Upaniṣadic phrases and words as "The Absolute is Consciousness-Bliss" (*Bṛ.Up.* III.ix.28.7), "A mere mass of Consciousness" (*Bṛ.Up.* II.iv.12), *Brahman*, *ātman*, the Absolute is artificially referred to with the help of

3. Huston Smith, *The World's Religions*, San Francisco: Harper. 1991, p. 34.

superimposed name, form and action, and spoken of exactly in the way we refer to objects of perception, as when we say "That white cow with horns is twitching". But if the desire is to express the true nature of the Absolute, void of all conditioning adjuncts and particularity, then it cannot be described by any positive means whatever. The only possible method then is to refer to it through a comprehensive denial of whatever positive characteristics have been attributed to it in previous teachings, and to say "neither this nor that" (*Bṛ.Up.Bhā.* II.III.6).

2. Nor can the Absolute be properly referred to by any such terms as "being" or "non-being". For all words are used to convey a meaning, and when heard by their hearers, convey the meaning the speaker had in mind. But communicable meaning is restricted without exception to universal, action, attribute and relation. . . . The Absolute, however, does not belong to any universal (genus), so it cannot be expressed by a noun such as "being" or "non-being". Being without attributes, it cannot be described by any adjective denoting any attribute. And being actionless, it cannot be expressed by any verb denoting activity. For the Upaniṣad speaks of it as "Without parts, without activity, at rest" (*Śvet.Up.* VI.19). Nor has it any relation with anything. For it is "One", "without a second", "not an object" and "the Self". Hence, it cannot be expressed by any word. And the Upaniṣadic texts themselves confirm this when they say "That from which words fall back" (*Taitt.Up.* II.9), and in other passages (*Bh.G.Bhā.* XIII.12).

3. The Absolute is that which ultimately has to be known. So, in order to show that it exists, it is first spoken of in its false form set-up by apparent conditioning

adjuncts, and fancifully referred to as if it had knowable attributes, in the words "with hands and feet everywhere". For there is the ancient maxim of those who know the tradition, "That which cannot be expressed in its true form (directly) is expressed (indirectly) through false attributes followed by retraction". And then the next verse of the *Gītā* is composed to make sure that it could not be supposed that the Absolute which is the object of our search truly had organs such as hands and feet, but mere adjuncts falsely attributed to it (*Bh.G.Bhā.* XIII.14, intro.).

— A.J. Alston[4]

4. A.J. Alston, tr., *The Method of the Vedanta: A Critical Account of the Advaita Tradition by Sri Swami Satchidanandendra Sarasvati*, London: Kegan Paul International, 1989, pp. 43-45.

2

Brahman: Nirguṇa and Saguṇa

The distinction as well as the interplay between the *nirguṇa* and the *saguṇa* aspects of *Brahman* is a persistent feature of Hinduism and this is brought out in section I. In section II the *saguṇa* aspect receives emphasis and in section III the *nirguṇa*. In section IV both are referred to indifferently.

I

This passage is a famous one, as it clearly affirms the monotheism underlying the deceptive polytheism encountered in Hinduism at the surface level. Yājñavalkya is a major thinker of the Upaniṣadic period.

1. Then Vidagdha Śākalya asked him: "How many gods are there, Yājñavalkya?" He answered, in accord with the following *nivid* (invocation of the gods), "As many as are mentioned in the *nivid* of the hymn of praise to the Viśvedevas, namely 303, and 3003." "Yes," Vidagdha said, "but how many gods are there, Yājñavalkya?" "Thirty three." "Yes," he said, "but how many gods are there, Yājñavalkya?" "Six." "Yes," said he, "but how many gods are there, Yājñavalkya?" "Two." "Yes," said he, "but how many gods are there, Yājñavalkya?" "One and a half." "Yes," said he, "but how many gods are there, Yājñavalkya?" "One." "Yes," said he, "but then which are those 303 and 3003?"
2. He (Yājñavalkya) said, "They are just the manifestations of them, but there are only thirty-three gods". "Which are these thirty-three?" "The eight Vasus, the eleven

Rudras, and the twelve Ādityas, these are thirty-one, Indra and Prajāpati (make up) thirty-three," replied Yājñavalkya.

3. "Which are the Vasus?" "The fire, the earth, the air, the sky, the sun, the heaven, the moon, the stars, these are the Vasus, for in them all this is placed, therefore they are called the Vasus."

4. "Which are the Rudras?" asked Vidagdha. "These ten breaths in a person with the mind as the eleventh. When they depart from this mortal body, they make us (his relatives) weep. So, because they make us weep, therefore they are called the Rudras."

5. "Which are the Ādityas?" To this Yājñavalkya replied, "Verily, the twelve months of the year, these are the Ādityas, for they move carrying along all this. Since they move carrying along all this, they are therefore called the Ādityas."

6. "Which is Indra? Which is Prajāpati?" "Indra is the thunder, Prajāpati is the sacrifice". "Which is the thunder?" "The thunderbolt." "Which is the sacrifice?" "The (sacrificial) animals."

7. "Which are the six?" "The fire, the earth, the air, the sky, the sun and the heaven, these are the six; for the six are all this."

8. "Which are the three gods?" Asked Vidagdha. "They are, verily, the three worlds, for in them all these gods exist." "Which are the two gods?" "Food and breath." "Which is the one and a half?" "This one here who blows (the air)."

9. "Regarding this, some say, since he who blows is like one, how then is he one and a half? (The answer is) because in him (when he blows) all this grew up."

"Which is the one God?" "The Breath. He is *Brahman*. They call him *tyat* (that)."

— *Bṛhadāraṇyaka Upaniṣad* III.9:1-9;
tr. S. Radhakrishnan[1]

II

Towards the end of the last passage the ultimate was identified with *Brahman* (neuter); in what follows it is referred to as *deva* and the concept is clearly and gloriously personal.

1. Some wise men speak of inherent nature, others likewise, of time (as the first cause), being deluded. But it is the greatness of God in the world, by which this *brahma-cakra* is made to turn.
2. He by whom this whole world is always enveloped, the knower, the author of time, the possessor of qualities and all knowledge. Controlled by Him (this) work (of creation) unfolds itself, that which is regarded as earth, water, fire, air and ether.
3. Having created this work and rested again, having entered into union with the essence of the self, by one, two, three or eight, or by time too and the subtle qualities of the self.
4. Who, having begun with works associated with the (three) qualities, distributes all existents. In the absence of these (qualities), there is the destruction of the work that has been done and in the destruction of the work he continues, in truth, other works (different from what he has produced).
5. He is the beginning, the source of the causes which unite (the soul with the body). He is to be seen as beyond the three kinds of time (past, present and

1. S. Radhakrishnan, ed., *The Principal Upaniṣads*, London: George Allen & Unwin Ltd., 1953, pp. 234-37.

future), and as without parts after having worshipped first that adorable God who has many forms, the origin of all beings, who abides in one's own thoughts.

6. Higher and other than the form of the world-tree and time is He from whom this world evolves, who brings good and removes evil, the lord of prosperity, having known Him as in one's own self, the immortal, the support of all (he attains *Brahman*).
7. He in whom is the Supreme Lord of lords, who is the highest deity of deities, the supreme master of masters, transcendent, Him let us know as God, the lord of the world, the adorable.
8. There is no action and no organ of His to be found. There is not seen his equal or his better. His high power is revealed to be various, indeed. The working of His intelligence and strength is inherent (in him).
9. Of Him there is no master in the world, no ruler, nor is there any mark of Him. He is the cause, the lord of the lords of the sense organs; of Him there is neither progenitor nor lord.
10. The one God who, according to His own nature, covers himself like a spider with threads produced from *pradhāna* (unmanifested matter), may He grant us entrance into *Brahman*.
11. The one God hidden in all beings, all-pervading, the inner-self of all beings, the ordainer of all deeds, who dwells in all beings, the witness, the knower, the only one, devoid of qualities.
12. The one controller of the many, inactive, who makes the one seed manifold. The wise, who perceive Him as abiding in their self, to them belongs eternal happiness, not to others.

13. He is the eternal among the eternals, the intelligent among the intelligences, the one among many, who grants desires. That cause which is to be apprehended by discrimination (of Sāṁkhya) and discipline (Yoga) — by knowing God, one is freed from all fetters.

14. The sun does not shine there, nor the moon and the stars, nor these lightnings, much less than fire. After Him, when He shines, everything shines, by His light all this is illumined.

15. The one bird in the midst of this world. This indeed is the fire that has entered into the ocean. Only by knowing Him does one pass over death. There is no other path for going there.

16. He is the maker of all, the knower of all, the self-caused, the knower, the author of time, the possessor of qualities, the knower of everything, the ruler of nature and of the spirit, the lord of qualities, the cause of worldly existence, and of liberation, of continuance and of bondage.

17. Becoming that, immortal, existing as the lord, the knower, the omnipresent, the guardian of this world is He who rules this world for ever, for no other cause is found for the ruling.

18. To Him who, of old, creates Brahmā and who, verily, delivers to him the Vedas, to that God who is lighted by His own intelligence, do I, eager for liberation, resort for refuge.

19. To him who is without parts, without activity, tranquil, irreproachable, without blemish, the highest bridge to immortality like a fire with its fuel burnt.

20. When men shall roll up space, as if it were a piece of leather, then will there be an end of sorrow, apart from knowing God.

21. By the power of austerity and the grace of God, the wise *Śvetāśvatara* in proper manner spoke about *Brahman*, the Supreme, the pure, to the advanced ascetics, what is pleasing to the company of seers.

22. This highest mystery in the Vedānta, which has been declared in a former age, should not be given to one whose passions are not subdued nor again to the one who is not a son or a pupil.

23. These subjects which have been declared shine forth to the high-souled one who has the highest devotion for God and for his spiritual teacher as for God. Yea they shine forth to the high-souled one.

— *Śvetāśvatara Upaniṣad* VI.1-23;
tr. by S. Radhakrishnan[2]

III

The following passage is in the form of a dialogue between Yājñavalkya and one of his wives, Maitreyī, at the end of which he renounces the householder's life — but not before he has answered her questions regarding *ātman = nirguṇa Brahman* in this context.

1. Now then, Yājñavalkya had two wives, Maitreyī and Kātyāyanī. Of the two, Maitreyī was a discourser on sacred knowledge (*brahmavādinī*); Kātyāyanī had just (*eva*) a woman's knowledge in that matter (*tarhi*).

   Now then, Yājñavalkya was about to commence another mode of life.

2. "Maitreyī!" said Yājñavalkya, "lo, verily, I am about to wander forth from this state. Behold! Let me make a final settlement for you and that Kātyāyanī."

3. Then spake Maitreyī: "If now, sir, this whole earth

2. S. Radhakrishnan, ed., *The Principal Upaniṣads*, London: George Allen & Unwin Ltd., 1953, pp. 743-50.

filled with wealth were mine, would I now thereby be immortal?"

"No, no!" said Yājñavalkya. "As the life of the rich, even so would your life be. Of immortality, however, there is no hope through wealth."

4. Then spake Maitreyī: "What should I do with that through which I may not be immortal? What you know, sir, that indeed, explain to me."

5. Then spake Yājñavalkya: "Though, verily, you, my lady, were dear to us, you have increased your dearness. Behold then, lady, I will explain it to you. But, while I am expounding, do you seek to ponder thereon."

6. Then spake he: "Lo, verily, not for love of the husband is a husband dear, but for love of the Soul (*ātman*) a husband is dear.

   Lo, verily, not for love of the wife is a wife dear, but for love of the Soul a wife is dear.

   Lo, verily, not for love of the sons are sons dear, but for love of the Soul sons are dear.

   Lo, verily, not for love of the wealth is wealth dear, but for love of the Soul wealth is dear.

   Lo, verily, not for love of the cattle are cattle dear, but for love of the Soul cattle are dear.

   Lo, verily, not for love of brāhmaṇahood is brāhmaṇahood dear, but for the love of the Soul brāhmaṇahood is dear.

   Lo, verily, not for love of kṣātrahood is kṣātrahood dear, but for love of the Soul kṣātrahood is dear.

   Lo, verily, not for love of the worlds are the worlds dear, but for love of the Soul the worlds are dear.

   Lo, verily, not for love of the gods are the gods dear, but for love of the Soul the gods are dear.

Lo, verily, not for love of the Vedas are the Vedas dear, but for love of the Soul the Vedas are dear.

Lo, verily, not for love of beings (*bhūta*) are beings dear, but for love of the Soul beings are dear.

Lo, verily, not for love of all is all dear, but for love of the Soul all is dear.

Lo, verily, it is the Soul (*Ātman*) that should be seen, that should be hearkened to, that should be thought on, that should be pondered on, O Maitreyī.

7. Brāhmaṇahood deserts him who knows brāhmaṇahood in aught else than the Soul. Kṣātrahood deserts him who knows kṣātṛahood in aught else than the Soul. The worlds desert him who knows the worlds in aught else than the Soul. The gods desert him who knows the gods in aught else than the Soul. The Vedas desert him who knows the Vedas in aught else than the Soul. Beings desert him who knows beings in aught else than the Soul. Everything deserts him who knows everything in aught else than the Soul. This brāhmaṇahood, this kṣātrahood, these worlds, these gods, these Vedas, all these beings, everything here is what this Soul is.

8. It is — as, when a drum is being beaten, one would not be able to grasp the external sounds, but by grasping the drum or the beater of the drum the sound is grasped.

9. It is — as, when a conch shell is being blown, one would not be able to grasp the external sounds, but by grasping the conch shell or the blower of the conch-shell the sound is grasped.

10. It is — as, when a lute is being played, one would not be able to grasp the external sounds, but by grasping the lute or the player of the lute the sound is grasped.

11. It is — as, from a fire laid with damp fuel, clouds of smoke separately issue forth, so, lo, verily, from this great being (*bhūta*) has been breathed forth that which is Ṛg-Veda, Yajur-Veda, Sāma-Veda, (hymns) of the Atharvans and Aṅgirases, legend (*itihāsa*), ancient lore (*purāṇa*), sciences (*vidyā*), mystic doctrines (*Upaniṣad*), verses (*śloka*), aphorisms (*sūtra*), explanations (*anuvyākhyāna*), commentaries (*vyākhyāna*), sacrifice, oblation, food, drink, this world and the other, and all beings. From it, indeed, have all these been breathed forth.

12. It is — as the uniting place of all waters is the sea, likewise the uniting-place of all touches is the skin; likewise the uniting-place of all tastes is the tongue; likewise the uniting-place of all odours is the nose; likewise the uniting-place of all forms is the eye; likewise the uniting-place of all sounds is the ear; likewise the uniting-place of all intentions is the mind; likewise the uniting-place of all knowledges is the heart; likewise the uniting-place of all actions is the hands; likewise the uniting-place of all pleasures is the generative organ; likewise the uniting-place of all evacuations is the anus; likewise the uniting-place of all journeys is the feet; likewise the uniting-place of all Vedas is the speech.

13. It is — as is a mass of salt, without inside, without outside, entirely a mass of taste, even so, verily, is this Soul, without inside, without outside, entirely a mass of knowledge.

    Arising out of these elements, into them also one vanishes away. After death there is no consciousness (*saṁjñā*). "Thus, lo, say I." Thus spake Yājñavalkya.

14. Then say Maitreyī: "Herein, indeed, you have caused

me, sir, to arrive at the extreme of bewilderment. Verily, I understand it (i.e. this *Ātman*) not."

Then said he: "Lo, verily, I speak not bewilderment. Imperishable, lo, verily, is this Soul, and of indestructible quality."

15. For where there is duality, as it were, there one sees another; there one smells another; there one tastes another; there one speaks to another; there one hears another; there one thinks of another; there one touches another; there one understands another. But where everything has become just one's own self, then whereby and whom would one see? then whereby and whom would one smell? then whereby and whom would one taste? then whereby and to whom would one speak? then whereby and whom would one hear? then whereby and of whom would one think? then whereby and whom would one touch? then whereby and whom would one understand? whereby would one understand Him by means of whom one understands this All?

That Soul (*Ātman*) is not this, it is not that (*neti, neti*). It is unseizable, for it cannot be seized; indestructible, for it cannot be destroyed; unattached, for it does not attach itself; it is unbound, does not tremble, is not injured.

Lo, whereby would one understand the understander?

Thus, you have the instruction told to you, Maitreyī. Such, lo, indeed, is immortality.

After speaking thus, Yājñavalkya departed.

— *Bṛhadāraṇyaka Upaniṣad* IV.5.1-15; tr. R.E. Hume[3]

3. Robert Ernest Hume, tr., *The Thirteen Principal Upanishads*, London: Oxford University Press, 1968; first published 1921, pp. 144-47.

IV

The issue of two forms of *Brahman* and what they might be called arises in the Upaniṣads itself, and the exact nature of the distinction involves constant clarification, as the ensuing points demonstrate.

We commence with an Upaniṣadic text:

1. Assuredly there are two forms of *Brahman*, the formed and the unformed, the mortal and the immortal, the static and the moving, the actual (*sat*) and the beyond (*tya*).
2. What is called the "formed" is (all) that is other than the wind and atmosphere. This is the mortal, the static, the actual. The essence of this formed, mortal, static, actual (*Brahman*) is [the sun] which gives out heat; for this is the essence of the actual.
3. Now, the unformed is the wind and atmosphere. This is the immortal, the moving, the beyond. The essence of this unformed, immortal, moving [*Brahman*] beyond is the Person in the disc [of the sun]; for this is the essence of the beyond. So much with regard to natural phenomena.
4. Now with regard to the self:

   The formed is what is other than the breath of life and the space within the self. This is the mortal, the static, the actual. The essence of this formed, mortal, static, actual [*Brahman*] is the eye; for this is the essence of the actual.
5. Now the unformed is the breath of life and the space within the self. This is the immortal, the moving, the beyond. The essence of this unformed, immortal, moving [*Brahman*] beyond is the Person in the right eye; for this is the essence of the beyond.

6. The form of this person is like a saffron-coloured robe, or like white wool, or an *indragopa* beetle, or a flame of fire, or a white lotus, or a sudden flash of lightning. Like a sudden flash of lightning too is the good fortune of the man who thus knows.

   From this follows the teaching (summed up in the words): "No, no!" For there is nothing higher than this "No". Or again, it can be named the "Real of the real". The life-breaths are the real and He is their Real.

   — *Bṛhadāraṇyaka Upaniṣad* II.3.1-6; tr. R.C. Zaehner[4]

In the commentarial material we find a constant effort to avoid a conflation of the two.

1. Are there two Absolutes, as supreme Absolute and a lower Absolute? Yes, there are two, as is shown by such texts as "This Absolute, O Satyakāma, in its supreme and lower aspects, in *oṁ*". — *Praśna* V.2

   What, then, is the supreme Absolute, and what the lower? To this we reply as follows. Where particularities arising from name and form set-up by ignorance are denied, and the Absolute is spoken of in negative terms such as "not gross, etc.", there we have the Supreme Absolute. When that same Absolute is referred to as qualified by some particular aspect of name and form for purposes of meditation, in such words as "Consisting of mind, having the vital energy for its body, luminous in nature" (*Chānd.* III.xiv.2), there we have the lower Absolute. But would not this contradict the texts affirming the non-duality of the Absolute? No. This objection stands refuted because the conditioning adjuncts are name and form set up by ignorance. — *B.S.Bhā.* IV.iii.14.

4. R.C. Zaehner, tr., *Hindu Scriptures*, New York: Dutton Everyman's Library, 1966 p. 44.

2. For, it is the supreme Absolute itself which is taught in some places only and for the sake of meditation, to be associated with conditioning adjuncts of a pure and elevating kind, and to have characteristics implying modification, such as "being composed of mind" (*Chānd.* III.xiv.2) and so on; in this context the Absolute is referred to as being "in its lower form (*apara*)".

   — *B.S.Bhā.* IV.iii.9

   It should not be supposed that this text is in conflict with the text "This Absolute, in its supreme and lower aspects, is *oṁ*" (*Praśna* V.2). For that latter text (was not a metaphysical statement but only) taught a meditation on *oṁ* conceiving it as the Absolute in its supreme form (the reward for which was liberation by stages). — Consult *B.S.Bhā.* I.iii.13

3. As for the difficulty that the Vedic texts also attribute to the Spirit a golden beard and the like, which is not compatible with his being the highest Lord, we reply to that as follows. The golden-bearded form could very well be one of those illusory forms deliberately assumed by the highest Lord for the sake of His devotees. For we have such a text from Smṛti as: "O Nārada, this that you behold is an illusion that I have projected. Do not suppose that in my true nature I am associated with the attributes of all creatures in this way". — Vyāsa, *Mbh.* XII.339.45

   Again, when the very highest form of the Lord is taught, with all particularities denied, we have such texts as "without sound, without touch, without form or colour, undecaying . . ." (*Kaṭha* I.iii.15). But sometimes the highest Lord, since He is the cause of all, is taught, for purposes of meditation, as having certain mutable characteristics. We have such texts on this subject as "He is the one acting in all activities, He is the one desiring in all good desires, He includes all odours and tastes" (*Chānd*. III.xiv.2). On this basis, texts teaching that He has a golden beard and the like are intelligible. — *B.S.Bhā*. I.ii.20

4. The teacher Bādari holds that the superhuman being conveys his charges to the Absolute in its lower form, associated with finite attributes (*Chānd*. IV.xv.5). This is because the Absolute in its (lower) form as effect has a particular position and so can be "reached". But one cannot conceive "goerhood" or "being gone to" or "the act of going" in relation to the Absolute in its highest form, for in this form it is all-pervasive and also the inmost Self of all "goers". — *B.S.Bhā*. IV.iii.7

5. We have already explained, in commenting on the *sūtra* "The soul is spoken of in this way (i.e. as atomic) when it is considered predominantly under the attributes of the intellect" (*B.S.* II.iii.29), that although the Self is all-pervasive, it has the appearance of movement when the intellect and other apparent conditioning adjuncts move, just as the ether of space appears to move with the movement of pots. — *B.S.Bhā*. IV.iii.14

6. Liberated souls have all supernatural powers, such as reducing their bodies to minute size, except that of producing, maintaining and withdrawing the universe. Those latter powers belong solely to the Lord, whose existence is eternal and self-evident. — *B.S.Bhā*. IV.iv.17

7. And so the identity with the Lord enjoyed by those liberated ones who still take their stand on the Absolute as modified into the world of effects (the Absolute in lower form) is not total. For the Veda (*Kauśītaki* I.7, *Bṛhad*. I.v.20,23) teaches that souls who are liberated

in this way have parity with the Lord, whose existence is beginningless and self-evident, only in point of enjoyment (not in respect of rulership of the universe).
— *B.S.Bhā.* IV.iv.21 — Tr. A.J. Alston.[5]

5. A.J. Alston, tr., op. cit., pp. 130-32.

3

Devī

The ultimate reality as *saguṇa* (with form), is imaged both in the female form and the male form in classical Hinduism. As this is not always the case in other religions, and may not have received sufficient recognition within the study of Hinduism itself, we identify it as the Goddess or Devī in this section, before identifying it as God or *Īśvara* in the next, thus imparting to the principle of "ladies first" — a divine dimension as it were.

The concept of the Devī as an independent goddess develops later, although seeds of it are present in the *Ṛg-Veda* and she is already beginning to gain divine status in the Upaniṣads. The first account is from the Upaniṣads; the second from a later source. The third citation shows the feminine theology of the Devī in full bloom.

I

The key nature of the passage becomes apparent only towards the end. In the end, "of the three — Agni, Vāyu and Indra — Indra obtained the knowledge that it was *Brahman* through the grace of Umā".[1]

Allegory of the Vedic God's Ignorance of Brahma

1. Now, Brahma won a victory for the gods. Now, in the victory of this Brahma the gods were exulting.

---

1. S. Radhakrishnan, ed., *The Principal Upaniṣads*, Atlantic Highlands, NJ, Humanities Press International, 1992 [1953], p. 590.

They bethought themselves: "Ours indeed is this victory! Ours indeed is this greatness!"

2. Now, It understood this of them. It appeared to them. They did not understand It, "What a wonderful being (*yakṣa*) is this?" they said.

3. They said to Agni (Fire): "Jātavedas, find out this — what this wonderful being is!"

   "So be it."

4. He ran unto It.

   Unto him It spoke: "Who are you?"

   "Verily, I am Agni," he said. "Verily, I am Jātavedas."

5. "In such as you what power is there?"

   "Indeed, I might burn everything here, whatever there is here in the earth!"

6. It put down a straw before him. "Burn that!"

   He went forth at it with all speed. He was not able to burn it. Thereupon, indeed he returned, saying: "I have not been able to find out this — what this wonderful being is."

7. Then they said to Vāyu (Wind): "Vāyu, find out this — what this wonderful being is!"

   "So be it."

8. He ran unto It.

   Unto him It spoke: "Who are you?"

   "Verily, I am Vāyu", he said. "Verily, I am Mātariśvan."

9. "In such as you what power is there?"

   "Indeed, I might carry off everything here, whatever there is here in the earth."

10. It put down a straw before him. "Carry that off!"

He went at it with all speed. He was not able to carry it off. Thereupon indeed he returned, saying: "I have not been able to find out this — what this wonderful being is."

11. Then they said to Indra: "Maghavan (Liberal), find out this — what this wonderful being is!"

"So be it."

He ran unto It. It disappeared from him.

12. In that very space he came upon a woman exceedingly beautiful, Umā, daughter of the snowy mountain (*Himavat*).

To her he said: "What is this wonderful being?"

1. "It is Brahma", she said. "In that victory of Brahma, verily, exult ye."

Thereupon he knew it was Brahma.

2. Therefore, verily, these gods, namely Agni, Vāyu, and Indra, are above the other gods, as it were; for these touched It nearest, for these and (especially) he (i.e. Indra) first knew It was Brahma.

3. Therefore, verily, Indra is above the other gods, as it were; for he touched It nearest, for he first knew It was Brahma.

— *Kena Upaniṣad* III.1-12; IV.1-3; tr. R.E. Hume.[2]

II

Umā, simply mentioned in the above Upaniṣad, is thus glorified as the Supreme Goddess in the later literature.

8. In the midst of the Ocean of Nectar, where covered with groves of heavenly wishing trees is the Isle of

---

2. Robert Ernest Hume, tr., *The Thirteen Principal Upanishads*, pp. 337-39.

Gems, in the mansion of wishing jewels with its grove of *nīpa* trees, on a couch composed of Śiva and the other gods, your seat a mattress which is Supreme Śiva — some few lucky ones worship you, a flood of consciousness and bliss.

12. To equal beauty, O daughter of the snowy mountain, master poets can scarcely succeed; the heavenly courtesans, when they have glimpsed it, through their longing to enjoy it, pass in imagination to identify with the mountain-dweller Śiva, who is hard to attain even by ascetic practices. . . .

21. Slender as a streak of lightning, composed of the essence of sun, moon, and fire, situated above the six lotuses, the manifestation of you in the forest of great lotuses, those with mind free of stain and illusion who view it, mighty ones, experience a flood of supreme joy.

22. "Do you, O Lady, extend to me, your slave, a compassionate glance!" — when one desiring to praise you utters the words "You, O Lady", at that moment you grant him a state of identity with you, with your feet illuminated by the crests of Viṣṇu, Brahmā, and Indra.

— Verses 8, 12, 21-22 of *Saundaryalaharī*;
tr. by W. Norman Brown[3]

III

The *locus classicus* of the worship of the Goddess is the *Devīmāhātmya,* which constitutes a part of the *Mārkaṇḍeya Purāṇa*. Of the three successful encounters of the Goddess with the demons narrated therein, perhaps her annihilation of demon Mahiṣa is the best known, and is recounted below:

---

3. As cited in Louis Renou, ed., *Hinduism,* New York: George Braziller, 1962, pp. 179-80.

The seer said:

2.1 In days of yore there was a battle between the *devas* and the *asuras* that lasted a full hundred years.

When Mahiṣa was chief of the *asuras* and Indra (chief) of the *devas*.

2.2 Then the army of the *devas* was conquered by the valorous *asuras*:

And having conquered all the gods, Mahiṣa became Indra (the chief).

2.3 Then the conquered gods, having put the lotus-born Prajāpati in front, went to the place where Śiva and Viṣṇu were.

2.4 The thirty (gods) told them of the extent of the gods' defeat; how it all happened, and likewise, the conduct of Mahiṣāsura.

2.5 "He himself now wields sovereignty over Sūrya, Indra, Agni, Vāyu, Candra, Yama, and over Varuṇa and the others.

2.6 All the hosts of gods, expelled from the heaven by the wicked Mahiṣa, wander on earth like (mere) mortals.

2.7 We have told you what the enemy of the gods has done, and we have taken refuge (in you). Please put your mind on doing away with him!"

2.8 Having heard these words of the gods, the slayer of Madhu (Viṣṇu) became angry, and Śiva too, with furrowed brows and twisted faces.

2.9 Then from Viṣṇu's face, which was filled with rage, came forth a great fiery splendour (*tejas*), (and also from the faces) of Brahmā and Śiva.

2.10 And from the bodies of the other gods, Indra and the others, came forth a great fiery splendour, and it became unified in one place.

2.11 An exceedingly fiery mass, like a flaming mountain, did the gods see there, filling the firmament with flames.

2.12 That peerless splendour, born from the bodies of all the gods, unified and pervading the triple world with its lustre, became a woman.

2.13 From Śiva's splendour her mouth was produced, her tresses from that of Yama, her arms from the splendor of Viṣṇu.

2.14 From that of Soma (the moon) came her two breasts, from that of Indra her waist, from that of Varuṇa her legs and thighs and from that of the earth her hips.

2.15 From the splendour of Brahmā her two feet (were produced), from the splendour of the sun her toes, From that of the Vasus her fingers, from that of Kubera her nose.

2.16 Her teeth were produced from the splendour of Prajāpati. And her three eyes came from the splendour of Agni.

2.17 Her eyes were the splendour of the two twilights, and her ears that of the wind, and whatever was born from the splendour of the other gods, that, too, was the auspicious (Goddess).

2.18 Having seen her, who was born from the rays of the splendour of all the gods, the gods who were tormented by Mahiṣa rejoiced.

2.19 Having withdrawn a trident from (his own) trident, Śiva gave it to her, and Kṛṣṇa gave her a discus, having pulled it out of his own discus.

2.20 And Varuṇa gave her a conch, Agni a spear, and Vāyu gave a bow and two quivers filled with arrows.

2.21 Indra, the lord of the immortals, (gave) a thunderbolt, having pulled it out of his own thunderbolt; the thousand-eyed one gave her a bell from his elephant, Airāvata.

2.22 From the staff of death, Yama gave a staff, Varuṇa a noose, and Prajāpati gave a string of beads, Brahmā an ascetic's waterjar.

2.23 The sun put his own rays into all the pores of her skin, and Kāla gave her a sword and spotless shield.

2.24 The sea of milk (gave) a flawless necklace and two unageing garments, a heavenly crest-jewel, two earrings and bracelets.

2.25 A heavenly half-moon (ornament), armlets on all her arms, two spotless anklets, likewise a neck-ornament without parallel.

2.26 And bejewelled rings on all her fingers.
Viśvakarmā gave her an utterly flawless axe.

2.27 Likewise, weapons of various forms, and unbreakable armour.

A garland of unwithering lotuses on her head, and another on her breast.

2.28 And an exceedingly brilliant lotus did the ocean give her.

The Himālaya (gave) a lion as her mount, and various jewels.

2.29 Kubera gave a drinking-cup filled with wine,

And Śeṣa, the lord of all snakes, who supports this earth:

2.30 Gave her a serpent-necklace, ornamented with great jewels. Honoured by the other gods with ornaments and weapons,

2.31 She bellowed out with laughter, again and again.

The entire atmosphere was filled with her terrible noise.

2.32 And with that measureless, overwhelming (noise) a great echo arose.

All the worlds quaked, and all the oceans shook.

2.33 The earth trembled, and mountains tottered.

And the gods, delighted, cried, "Victory!" to her whose mount is a lion.

2.34 And sages praised her, their bodies bowed in devotion.

Having seen the triple world trembling, the enemies of the gods;

2.35 With all their armies prepared for the battle, their weapons upraised, rose up together.

Mahiṣāsura, having fumed in anger, cried "Ah, what is this?"

2.36 Rushed toward the sound, surrounded by all the *asuras*.

Then he saw the Goddess, filling the triple world with her radiance.

2.37 Causing the earth to bow down at the tread of her feet, scratching the sky with her diadem.

Making all the nether regions tremble at the sound of her bowstring;

2.38 Standing (there) filling all the directions with her thousand arms. Then there began a battle between the Goddess and the enemies of the gods.

2.39 With the atmosphere illuminated by the weapons and the missiles that were hurled in abundance.

The great Asura Cikṣura, Mahiṣāsura's general,

2.40 Fought, and Cāmara, outfitted with an army of four divisions, along with others,

The great *asura* named Udagra, with 60,000 chariots.

2.41 Mahāhanu with 10 million fighting,

The great *asura* Asiloman with fifty million.

2.42 Bāṣkala fought in the battle with 60 million (chariots), Parivārita with many multitudes of thousands of elephants and horses.

2.43 Surrounded in battle by 10 million (chariots), the one named Viḍāla

Fought, with 5 billion (chariots).

2.44 He fought in the battle there, surrounded with chariots,

And myriads of others surrounded by chariots, elephants, and horses.

2.45 (All the) great Asuras fought there in that battle with the Goddess,

With countless chariots and elephants.

2.46 And horses surrounded, Mahiṣāsura was there in the battle. With iron maces and javelins, with spears and cudgels.

2.47 With swords, battleaxes, and pikes they fought with the Goddess in the battle.

Some threw spears, while others (threw) nooses.

2.48 They attacked the Goddess in order to slay her with blows from their clubs.

These weapons and arms the Goddess Caṇḍikā,

2.49 Broke as if in play, showering down her own weapons and arms.

The Goddess, being praised by gods and seers, appeared unruffled.

2.50 The queen released weapons and arms at the bodies of the Asuras.

The lion-mount of the Goddess, with a shaken mane, angry;

2.51 Roamed among the armies of the Asuras, like fire in the forest.

The breaths that Ambikā released while fighting in the battle.

2.52 These immediately became her hosts, by the hundreds and thousands.

They fought with axes, javelins, swords, and pikes.

2.53 Sustained by the power of the Goddess, destroying the *asura* hordes.

Some of her throng caused battledrums to resound, and others conches.

2.54 And still others tabors in the great festival of the battle.

Then the Goddess with her tridents, clubs, and shower of spears.

2.55 With sword and the like slew the great *asura*s by the hundreds.

And she felled others who were deluded by the sound of her bell.

2.56 And having bound some Asuras on the ground with her noose, she dragged them along.

Others were cut in two by the sharp blows from her sword.

2.57 Still others, crushed by the fall of her club, lay on the ground,

And some, much smitten by her mace, vomitted blood.

2.58 Some fell to the ground, their chests rent by her spear.
Others were destroyed on the field of battle, cut by the flood of arrows.

2.59 (Merely) a semblance of an army, those tormentors of the gods breathed their last.

The arms of some were broken, and others had broken necks.

2.60 The heads of some fell (to the ground), others were pierced in the middle.

And other great Asuras, with their legs cut-off, fell to the earth.

2.61 Others were cut in half by the Goddess, having (in each part) a single arm, an eye, and a leg.

Some, when their heads were cut-off, fell (and) rose again.

2.62 Headless trunks, (still) grasping the best of weapons, fought with the Goddess.

And others danced in the battle, keeping time to the sound of the drums.

2.63 Headless trunks, with broken heads, with sword, spear, and double-edged sword still in hand.

Other great Asuras cried out, "Stop! Stop!" to the Goddess.

2.64 The earth became impassable with the fallen chariots, elephants, horses, and Asuras,

Which had come together there where the great battle occurred.

2.65 Great rivers with torrents of blood from the elephants, Asuras, and horses,

Flowed there in the midst of the Asura army.

2.66 Thus did Ambikā lead to destruction the great army of the Asuras,

Just as a great fire dries a pie of grass and wood.

2.67 And (her) lion, tossing its mane and uttering a terrible roar,

Rooted around searching for breaths still coming from the bodies of the enemies of the gods.

2.68 In this way did the battle take place between the *asuras* and the hosts of the Goddess,

So that the gods were pleased with them, releasing showers of flowers from the heaven.

The seer said:

3.1 Having seen his army being slain, the great Asura General Cikṣura went forth in anger to fight Ambikā.

3.2 The Asura rained a shower of arrows on the Goddess in battle,

Just as a cloud showers the summit of Mount Meru with rain.

3.3 The Goddess, having broken his multitudes of arrows just in play,

Killed the horses and the driver of the horses with (her) arrows.

3.4 And straightaway she broke his bow and upraised banner,

And she pierced the limbs of the broken-bowed one with arrows.

3.5 With his bow broken, without chariot, with his horses slain, and his charioteer dead,

The Asura ran at the Goddess, armed with sword and shield.

3.6 Having hit the lion on the head with a sharp-edged sword,

He of great speed struck the Goddess on the left arm.

3.7 On touching her arm, the sword exploded, O prince. Then he seized his lance, his eyes red with anger.

3.8 The great Asura then hurled the flaming (weapon) at Bhadrakālī

As if it were the disc of the sun with shimmerings from the sky.

3.9 On seeing the flying lance, the Goddess released (her own) lance.

By it, the Asura's weapon, was shattered into 100 pieces, and the great *asura*, too.

3.10 When the valorous leader of Mahiṣa's army was slain,

The afflicter of the gods (named) Cāmara came forward, mounted on an elephant.

3.11 He released a spear at the Goddess. Ambikā quickly caused it to

Fall to the ground splendourless, dashed by her roar.

3.12 Having seen his spear fall shattered filled, with anger, Cāmara hurled a lance. Even it she broke with her arrows.

3.13 Then (her) lion, rising up, fastened on the space between the frontal lobes of the elephant,

In hand-to-paw combat he fought fiercely with (Cāmara), the enemy of the gods.

3.14 The fighting pair fell from the elephant to the earth. Locked in battle the two fought with dreadful blows.

3.15 Then having leapt up into the sky and descended (again) quickly,

The lion severed Cāmara's head with a blow from his paw.

3.16 Udagra was slain in battle by the Goddess with rocks, trees, and so forth.

And Karāla was felled with her teeth, fists, and palm.

3.17 The angry Goddess pulverised Uddhata with blows from her club,

Bāṣkala with her javelin, and Tāmra (and) Andhaka with arrows.

3.18 The supreme Goddess with her trident slew

Ugrāsya and Ugravīrya and likewise Mahāhanu.

3.19 She caused Biḍāla's head to fall from his body with her sword;

She led both Durdhara and Durmukha to the abode of death with arrows.

3.20 When his own army was thus destroyed, Mahiṣāsura

In his own buffalo form, caused (the goddess's) troops to tremble.

3.21 Some (he slew) with the blow of his snout, others with the stampings of his hooves;

Others (were) lashed with his tail, still others torn by his horns.

3.22 Others by his (sheer) speed, his bellow, his wheeling about,

Still others by the wind of his breaths did he knock to the surface of the earth.

3.23 Having cast down the hosts of Pramathas, the Asura,

Ran forth to slay the great Goddess's lion. Then Ambikā became infuriated.

3.24 In anger he of great valour, pounding the earth with his hooves,

Hurled up mountains with his horns and bellowed.

3.25 The earth, trampled by his rapid whirlings, was crushed,

And the ocean, flailed by his tail, flooded everywhere.

3.26 Clouds were torn in pieces, rent by his swaying horns,

Mountains by the hundreds, thrown about by his breath, fell from the sky.

3.27 Having seen the great onrushing Asura, inflated with anger,

Caṇḍikā got angry in order to slay him.

3.28 Hurling a snare at him, she bound the great Asura. Thus bound in the great battle, he abandoned his buffalo form.

3.29 Immediately thereupon he became a lion. As soon as Ambikā cut-off his head,

He appeared as a man, with sword in hand.

3.30 Instantly the Goddess cut the man to shreds with his arrows,

Along with his sword and shield. Then he became a great elephant.

3.31 With his trunk he dragged the great lion and roared;

The Goddess cut-off the trunk of the dragging one with her sword.

3.32 At this point, the great Asura resumed his buffalo form again.

Thus, he caused the three worlds, along with what does and does not move, to tremble.

3.33 Then the angry Caṇḍikā, mother of the world, quaffed a superior beverage,

And again and again she laughed, with reddened eyes.

3.34 The Asura, puffed up and drunk with might and power, bellowed

And with his horns hurled mountains at Caṇḍikā.

3.35 Pulverising what he threw with a volley of arrows,

With passion in her face that was flushed with intoxication, she uttered fevered words.

The Goddess said:

3.36 "Roar, roar for a moment, O fool, while I drink (this) nectar!

When you are slain here by me, it is the gods who soon will roar!"

The seer said:

3.37 Having spoken thus and springing up, she mounted the great Asura. Having struck him with her foot, she beat him with her spear.

3.38 Then he, struck with her foot, came forth out of his own mouth,

Completely hemmed in by the valour of the Goddess.

3.39 That great Asura, who had come forth halfway fighting, was felled by the Goddess,

Who had cut-off his head with a great sword.

3.40 Then the whole demon army, crying "Alas, alas!" perished,

And all the throngs of gods attained the highest bliss.

3.41 The gods together with the great heavenly seers praised the Goddess.

The leaders of the Gandharvas sang, and throngs of Apsarases danced.

The seer said:

4.1 When the exceedingly brave (and) wicked (Mahiṣa) and the army of the enemies of the gods were slain by the Goddess, throngs of gods, led by Indra,

Praised her with their voices, their necks and

shoulders bowed in reverence, their bodies made beautiful by shuddering in ecstasy.

4.2 "To the Goddess by whom this world was spread out through her own power, whose body is comprised of the powers of all the hosts of gods,

To Ambikā, worthy of worship by all gods and great seers, are we bowed down in devotion; may she bring about auspicious things for us.

4.3 May she whose peerless splendour and might the blessed Viṣṇu, Brahmā, and Śiva cannot describe,

May she, Caṇḍikā, fix her mind on the protection of the entire world, and on the destruction of the fear of evil.

4.4 May she who is Śrī herself in the abodes of those who do good, Alakṣmī (in the abodes) of those whose soul is wicked, intelligence in the hearts of the wise,

Faith (in the hearts) of the good, modesty (in the heart of) one of good birth, to you who are she are we bowed down: protect the universe, O Goddess!

4.5 How can we describe this unthinkable form of yours? Or your abundant, surpassing valour which destroys Asuras?

Or such deeds as (you do) in battles among all the throngs of Asuras and gods, O Goddess?

4.6 (You are) the cause of all the worlds; although possessed of the three qualities (*guṇa*s), by faults you are now known; (you are) unfathomable even by Hari, Hara and the other gods.

(You are) the resort of all, (you are) this entire world that is composed of parts, for you are the supreme, original, untransformed Prakr̥ti.

4.7 By means of whose utterance, every deity attains satisfaction at all sacrifices, O Goddess,

You are Svāhā, and, (as) the cause of satisfaction of the multitude of Manes, you are proclaimed by men to be Svadhā.

4.8 You who are the cause of release and of inconceivable austerities, your name is repeated by sages, who hold the essence of truth because they have restrained their senses,

Intent upon *mokṣa* with all faults shed: you are this blessed, supreme knowledge, O Goddess.

4.9 Having sound as your very soul, the resting-place of the utterly pure *Ṛg* and *Yajur* (hymns) and of the *Sāmans*, delightfully recited with the *udgītha*,

The Goddess (are you), the blessed triple (Veda), acting for the existence and production of all worlds, the supreme destroyer of pain.

4.10 O Goddess, you are the insight, knowing the essence of all scriptures, you are Durgā, a vessel upon the ocean of life (that is so) hard to cross, devoid of attachments.

(You are) Śrī, whose sole abode is in the heart of Kaiṭabha's foe (Viṣṇu); you are Gaurī, whose abode is made with the one who is crowned with the moon (Śiva).

4.11 Slightly smiling, spotless, like the orb of the full moon, as pleasing as the lustre of the finest god (is your face).

Wondrous it is that when the Asura Mahiṣa saw (this) face, he suddenly struck it, his anger aroused.

4.12 But O Goddess, the fact that Mahiṣa, having seen (your face) angry, terrible with knitted brows, in hue like the rising moon, did not immediately

Give up his life is exceedingly wondrous — for who can live, having seen death enraged?

4.13 O Goddess, may you, the supreme one, be gracious to life; enraged, you (can) destroy (whole) families in a trice.

This is now known, since the extensive power of the Asura Mahiṣa has been brought to an end.

4.14 Honoured are they among nations, riches are theirs, honours are theirs, and their portion of *dharma* does not fail,

Fortunate are they, with devoted children, servants, and wives, on whom you, the gracious one, always bestow good fortune.

4.15 O Goddess, a virtuous man always attentively performs all righteous actions on a daily basis,

And then he goes to the heaven by your grace: are you not thus the bestower of rewards on the three worlds, O Goddess?

4.16 O Durgā, (when) called to mind, you take away fear from every creature; (when) called to mind by the healthy, you bestow an exceedingly pure mind.

O you who destroy poverty, misery, and fear, who other than you is always tender-minded, in order to work benefits for all?

4.17 Since these (foes) are slain, the world attains happiness; although they have committed (enough) sin to remain in the hell for a long time,

It is with the thought — "Having met death in battle, may they go to the heaven" — that you assuredly slay (our) enemies, O Goddess.

4.18 Having, in fact, seen them, why do you not (immediately) reduce all the Asuras to ashes, since you hurl your weapon at enemies?

"Let even enemies, purified by (my) weapons, attain (heavenly) worlds" — such is your most gracious intent even toward those who are hostile.

4.19 Although the eyes of the Asuras were not destroyed by the terrible flashings of the light-mass of your sword, or by the abundant lustre of your spearpoint,

While they looked at your face, which was like a portion of the radiant moon, that very thing happened (i.e. their eyes were destroyed).

4.20 Your disposition, O Goddess, calms the activity of evildoers, and this incomprehensible form (of yours) is unequalled by others,

And (your) valour slays those who have robbed the gods of their prowess: thus was compassion shown by you even towards enemies.

4.21 With what may this prowess of yours be compared? Where is there (such a) form, exceedingly charming (yet) striking fear into enemies?

Compassion in mind and severity in battle are seen in you, O Goddess, who bestow boons upon the triple world.

4.22 This whole world was rescued by you, through the destruction of (its) enemies; having slain (them) at the peak of the battle,

The hosts of enemies were led to the heaven by you, and your fear, arising from the frenzied foes of the gods, was dispelled: hail to you!

4.23 With (your) spear protect us, O Goddess! And with (your) sword protect (us), O Ambikā!

Protect us with the sound of (your bell), and with the twang of your bowstring!

4.24 In the east protect (us) and in the west, O Caṇḍikā; protect (us) in the north

By the wielding of your spear, likewise in the north, O Queen.

4.25 With your gentle forms that roam about in the triple world,

And with the exceedingly terrible ones, protect us, and also the earth.

4.26 And with the weapons, O Ambikā, sword, and spear, and club, and the rest,

Which lie in your sprout (-like) hands, protect (us) on every side."

The seer said:

4.27 Thus was the supportress of the world praised by the gods with heavenly flowers growing in Indra's pleasure garden,

And praised with perfumes and ointments.

4.28 With devotion was she censed by all the 30 (gods) with heavenly incenses.

With gracious face she spoke to all the prostrate gods.

The Goddess said:

4.29 "O all (you) thirty (gods), whatever is desired from us, let that be chosen.

[I (will) gladly give (it since I am) well worshipped with these hymns of praise."]

The gods said:

"All has been done by You. Nothing is left,

4.30 Since this enemy of ours, Mahiṣāsura, was slain.
But if a boon is to be given to us by you, O great queen,

4.31 (Let it be that) whenever you are remembered by us, may you destroy (our) greatest misfortunes.

And whatever mortal praises you with these hymns, O one whose face is without blemish.

4.32 May you, O Ambikā, who are resorted to by us, the grantress of everything,

Be concerned with his growth through wealth, wife, success, (etc.) by means of riches, prosperity, and power."

The seer said:

4.33 Thus graciously solicited by the gods both for their own well-being and for that of the world, having said, "I consent," Bhadrakālī disappeared, O king.

4.34 Thus has it been related, O king, how she, the Goddess, was formerly produced from the bodies of the gods, desiring the well-being of the three worlds.

— *Devīmāhātmya* 2.1-4.34; tr. Thomas Coburn.[4]

IV

The divinisation of the feminine principle even led to the suggestion that spiritual goals were more accessible to women than to men, as in some forms of Tantra. The following verse is quoted by Jayaratha in his commentary on the *Tantrāloka* of Abhinavagupta, the foremost exponent of Kāśmīra Śaivism:

That attainment, which is said to be achieved in one year's time by those terrified, is achieved in 12 days by those divine ladies who are established in Śaivism.[5]

V

We conclude this chapter with a famous hymn which hails the Goddess.

---

4. Thomas B. Coburn, *Encountering the Goddess: A Translation of the Devīmāhātmya and Study in Its Interpretation,* Albany, N.Y.: State University of New York Press, 1991, pp. 39-52.

5. Swami Lakshman Joo, *Kashmir Shaivism: The Secret Supreme,* ed. John Hughes, Albany, New York: State University of New York Press [The Universal Shaiva Trust], 1988, p. 107, n. 2.

The gods said:

5.7 "Hail to the Goddess, hail eternally to the auspicious great Goddess!

Hail to Prakṛti, the auspicious! We who are restrained bow down to her.

5.8 To the terrible one, hail! To the eternal Gaurī, the supportress, hail!

And to the moonlight, to the blissful one having the form of the moon, hail eternally!

5.9 To the auspicious one (are we) bowed down; to growth, to success, to Kūrmī, alleluia, alleluia!

To Nairṛti, to the Lakṣmī of kings, to you, Śarvāṇī, hail, hail!

5.10 To Durgā, the inaccessible further shore, the essential one who accomplishes all,

To fame, likewise the black one, the smokey one, hail eternally!

5.11 To the one who is exceedingly gentle and exceedingly terrible (are we) bowed down: hail, hail!

Hail to the support of the world, to the Goddess (who is) action: hail, hail!

5.12 The Goddess who is known as the *māyā* of Viṣṇu in all creatures,

Hail to her, hail to her, hail to her: hail, hail!

5.13 The Goddess who is designated "consciousness" in all creatures,

Hail to her, hail to her, hail to her: hail, hail!

5.14 The Goddess who abides in all creatures in the form of intelligence,

Hail to her, hail to her, hail to her: hail, hail!

5.15 The Goddess who abides in all creatures in the form of sleep,

Hail to her, hail to her, hail to her: hail, hail!

5.16 The Goddess who abides in all creatures in the form of hunger,

Hail to her, hail to her, hail to her: hail, hail!

5.17 The Goddess . . . shadow,

Hail to her, hail to her, hail to her: hail, hail!

5.18 The Goddess . . . power,

Hail to her, hail to her, hail to her: hail, hail!

5.19 The Goddess . . . thirst,

Hail to her, hail to her, hail to her: hail, hail!

5.20 The Goddess . . . patience,

Hail to her, hail to her, hail to her: hail, hail!

5.21 The Goddess . . . birth,

Hail to her, hail to her, hail to her: hail, hail!

5.22 The Goddess . . . modesty,

Hail to her, hail to her, hail to her: hail, hail!

5.23 The Goddess . . . tranquillity,

Hail to her, hail to her, hail to her: hail, hail!

5.24 The Goddess . . . faith,

hail to her, hail to her, hail to her: hail, hail!

5.25 The Goddess . . . loveliness,

Hail to her, hail to her, hail to her: hail, hail!

5.26 The Goddess . . . Lakṣmī,

Hail to her, hail to her, hail to her: hail, hail!

5.27 The Goddess . . . activity,

Hail to her, hail to her, hail to her: hail, hail!

5.28 The Goddess . . . memory,

Hail to her, hail to her, hail to her: hail, hail!

5.29 The Goddess . . . compassion,

Hail to her, hail to her, hail to her: hail, hail!

5.30 The Goddess . . . contentment,

Hail to her, hail to her, hail to her: hail, hail!

5.31 The Goddess . . . mother,

Hail to her, hail to her, hail to her: hail, hail!

5.32 The Goddess . . . error,

Hail to her, hail to her, hail to her: hail, hail!

5.33 She who is the inner controller of the senses in all creatures,

And constantly in the elements, to the Goddess who is the fact of universal presence, hail, hail!

5.34 She who abides, having pervaded this whole world in the form of mind.

Hail to her, hail to her, hail to her: hail, hail!

5.35 Praised of yore by the gods because refuge was desired, similarly, praised by the lord of gods day after day,

May she, the queen, the cause of what is bright, accomplish for us bright things, auspicious things: may she destroy misfortunes.

5.36 She, the ruler, is now reverenced by us, the gods, who are tormented by haughty demons.

And at this very moment, she who has been called to mind by us, whose bodies are prostrated in devotion, destroys all misfortunes.

— *Devīmāhātmya* 5.7-5.36: tr. Thomas Coburn[6]

---

6. Thomas Coburn, op. cit., pp. 53-55.

4

Īśvara

I

The extract which follows is from the *Īśa Upaniṣad* — usually mentioned first in the traditional enumeration of the Upaniṣads. In fact, the extract is the Upaniṣad — consisting as it does of 18 verses. This Upaniṣad seems to combine the two sources of the concept of Īśvara as identified by M. Hiriyanna; the monotheism which emerges "from the polytheism of the *mantras*",[1] and the monotheism which has its roots in the monism of the Upaniṣads, which "is directly derived from the *Brahman–Ātman* conception and, in consonance with it" takes the Supreme God "to be immanent in all that constitutes the universe, including gods and men".[2]

Recognition of the Unity Underlying the Diversity of the World

1. By the Lord (*Īśa*) enveloped must this all be —
Whatever moving thing there is in the moving world.
With this renounced, thou mayest enjoy.
Covet not the wealth of anyone at all.

Non-attachment of Deeds on the Person of a Renouncer

2. Even while doing deeds here,
One may desire to live a hundred years.
Thus on thee — not otherwise than this is it —

1. M. Hiriyanna, *The Essentials of Indian Philosophy*, London: George Allen & Unwin, 1948, p. 30.
2. Ibid.

The deed (*karman*) adheres not on the man.

The Forbidding Future for Slayers of the Self

3. Devilish (*asurya*) are those worlds called,
With blind darkness (*tamas*) covered o'er!
Unto them, on deceasing, go
Whatever folk are slayers of the Self.

The All-Surpassing, Paradoxical World-Being

4. Unmoving, the One (*ekam*) is swifter than the mind.
The sense-powers (*deva*) reached not It, speeding on before.
Past others running, This goes standing.
In It Mātariśvan places action.

5. It moves. It moves not.
It is far, and It is near.
It is within all this,
And It is outside of all things.

6. Now, he who on all beings
Looks as just (*eva*) in the Self (*ātman*),
And on the Self as in all beings —
He does not shrink away from Him.

7. In whom all beings
Have become just (*eva*) the Self of the discerner —
Then what delusion (*moha*), what sorrow (*śoka*) is there
Of him who perceives the unity!

Characteristics of the World-ruler

8. He has environed. The bright, the bodiless, the scatheless,
The sinewless, the pure (*śuddha*), unpierced by evil (*a-pāpa-viddha*)!
Wise (*kavi*), intelligent (*manīṣin*), encompassing (*paribhū*), self-existent (*svayambhū*),

Appropriately he distributed objects (*artha*) through
the eternal years.

Transcending, While Involving, the Antithesis of Knowing

9. Into blind darkness enter they
That worship ignorance;
Into darkness greater than that, as it were, they
That delight in knowledge.

10. Other, indeed, they say, than knowledge!
Other, they say, than non-knowledge!
— Thus we have heard from the wise (*dhīra*)
Who to us have explained it.

11. Knowledge and non-knowledge —
He who is pair conjointly (*saha*) knows,
With non-knowledge passing over death,
With knowledge wins the immortal.

The Inadequacy of Any Antithesis of Being

12. Into blind darkness enter they
Who worship non-becoming (*a-sambhūti*);
Into darkness greater than that, as it were, they
Who delight in becoming (*sambhūti*).

13. Other, indeed — they say — than origin (*sambhava*)!
Other — they say — than non-origin (*a-sambhava*)!
— Thus have we heard from the wise
Who to us have explained It.

Becoming and Destruction a Fundamental Duality

14. Becoming (*sambhūti*) and destruction (*vināśa*) —
He who this pair conjointly (*saha*) knows,
With destruction passing over death,
With becoming wins the immortal.

A Dying Person's Prayer

15. With a golden vessel
The Real's face is covered o'er
That do thou, O Pūṣan, uncover
For one whose law is the Real to see.

16 O Nourisher (*pūṣan*), the sole Seer (*ekarṣi*), O Controller (*yama*), O Sun (*sūrya*), offspring of Prajāpati, spread forth thy rays! Gather thy brilliance (*tejas*)! What is thy fairest form — that of thee I see. He who is yonder, yonder Person (*puruṣa*) — I myself am he!

17. [My] breath (*vāyu*) to the immortal wind (*anila*)! This body then ends in ashes! *Oṁ*!

O Purpose (*kratu*), remember! The deed (*kṛta*) remember!

O Purpose, remember! The deed remember!

General Prayer of Petition and Adoration

18. O Agni, by a goodly path to prosperity (*rai*) lead us,
Thou god who knowest all the ways!
Keep far from us crooked-going sin (*enas*)!
Most ample expression of adoration to thee would we render!
— Tr. R.E. Hume[3]

II

That the ultimate reality (*Brahman*) must be ultimately understood as *saguṇa Brahman*; that is to say, as *Īśvara* or God is the conclusive opinion of Rāmānuja (twelfth century). He expounds his thesis as follows in his *Vedārtha-Saṁgraha*:

> Our thesis about the Reality and the ways of knowing can be formulated in this way: The Supreme *Brahman* is by its

---

3. Robert Ernest Hume, tr., op. cit., pp. 362-65.

inherent nature antithetical to all imperfections. Its substantive nature consists solely of infinite knowledge and bliss. It is an ocean of exalted attributes which are natural to it and are all-surpassing in their excellence. Its glories are boundless and not tainted by mutations in time, time which is the operative principle of change in the form of origination, subsistence and destruction and consists of limitless number of units, like seconds, minutes, hours up to vast epochs. *Brahman* has, as the instruments of its mighty sport and as forming its own parts, an infinite number of individual souls bound as well as free and also the physical universe, which latter has the power of passing through evolutions, marvellous and boundless. *Brahman* is the inner ruler of the finite selves and the non-sentient nature. They form its body. It owns them as its modes. Such Supreme *Brahman* is the reality to be known. The Veda, *Ṛk*, *Yajur*, *Sāman* and *Atharvan*, branching forth thousandfold, beginningless and endless in its unbroken tradition, embodying the ultimate truth, is the basis of philosophical knowledge. This, in all its three sections, namely injunctions, explanations and hymns, is supported and interpreted by the Itihāsas, Purāṇas, and Dharmaśāstras, composed by the great sages, like Bhagavān Dvaipāyana, Parāśara, Vālmīki, Manu, Yājñavalkya, Gautama and Āpastamba, who have attained the direct vision of the Supreme *Brahman*. This body of transcendent knowledge, interpreted and augmented in the supplementary sacred texts of these perfect sages, is the final authority. Can there be any insuperable difficulty for us, possessed of this magnificent conception of knowledge and reality? — Tr. S.S. Raghavachar[4]

4. S.S. Raghavachar, tr., *Vedārtha-Saṁgraha of Śrī Rāmānujācārya*, Mysore: Sri Ramakrishna Mission, 1968, p. 41.

5

Trimūrti

The concept of Trimūrti is clearly identifiable in the *Maitrī Upaniṣad*. The relevant passage, cited below, starts out by enumerating the three gods but proceeds to identify the unitary divinity with a host of other gods as well. In the second movement, however, as represented by the second passage, the "trinitarian" aspect is identified, though it is perhaps typical of Hinduism that it does not stop at three!

The Conception of Trimūrti

1. Now then this is Kutsāyana's hymn of praise:

   Thou art Brahmā and verily thou art Viṣṇu, thou art Rudra and thou Prajāpati; thou art Agni, Varuṇa, Vāyu, thou art Indra and thou art the moon. Thou art food, thou art Yama, thou art the earth, thou art all, thou art the Imperishable. All things exist in thee in many forms for their own or for their natural ends. Lord of the universe, salutations to thee, the self of all, the maker of all, the enjoyer of all, thou art all life and the lord of all pleasure and delight. Salutations to thee, the tranquil self, salutations to thee, the deeply hidden, the incomprehensible, the immeasurable and without beginning and without end.

2. Verily, in the beginning this (world) was darkness alone. That was in the Highest. When impelled by the Highest it moves on to differentiation. That form, verily, is passion. That passion, when impelled, moves on to differentiation. That, verily, is the form of

goodness. That goodness, when impelled, the essence flowed forth. That part is what the intelligence principle in every person is, the knower of the body, which has the marks of conception, determination and self-love, Prajāpati (the lord of creation) called Viśva. His forms have been previously mentioned. Now then, indeed the part of him which is characterised by darkness that, O students of sacred knowledge, is this Rudra. Now then, indeed, that part of him which is characterised by passion, that, O students of sacred knowledge, is this Brahmā. Now then, indeed, that part of him which is characterised by goodness, that, O students of sacred knowledge, is this Viṣṇu. Verily, that one becomes threefold. He developed forth eightfold, elevenfold, twelvefold, in unlimited parts. Because he thus developed, he is a (created) being, he moves about, having entered all beings. He became the lord of (created) beings. That is the self within and without, yea, within and without.

— *Maitrī Upaniṣad* V.1-2; tr. S. Radhakrishnan[1]

---

1. S. Radhakrishnan, ed., *The Principal Upaniṣads*, Atlantic Heights, NJ, Humanities Press International, 1992 [1953], pp. 814-15.

6

Brahmā

Sometimes the Upaniṣads are characterised as absolutistic or theistic, depending on whether they are prevailingly absolutistic or theistic. The theistic Upaniṣads, in turn, are sometimes identified by the god of the Trimūrti who is preeminent in them. From this standpoint the *Muṇḍaka Upaniṣad* may be associated with Brahmā, the *Kaṭha Upaniṣad* with Viṣṇu, and the *Śvetāśvatara Upaniṣad* with Śiva.

What follow are some extracts from the *Muṇḍaka Upaniṣad* pertaining to Brahmā.

I

In this passage Brahmā appears virtually as the original *guru*:

1. Brahmā arose as the first among the gods, the maker of the universe, the protector of the world. He taught the knowledge of *Brahman*, the foundation of all knowledges, to Atharvaṇa, his eldest son.
2. That knowledge of *Brahman*, which Brahmā taught to Atharvaṇa, and Atharvaṇa in olden times told Aṅgiras. He (in his turn) taught it to Satyavāha, son of Bhāradvāja and the son of Bhāradvāja to Aṅgiras — both the higher and the lower (knowledge).

— *Muṇḍaka Upaniṣad* I.1.1-2; tr. S. Radhakrishnan[1]

---

1. S. Radhakrishnan, ed., *The Principal Upaniṣads*, Atlantic Heights, NJ, Humanities Press International, 1992 [1953], p. 671.

II

In these passages Brahmā's relationship to *Brahman* is alluded to:

6. That which is ungraspable, without family, without caste, without sight or hearing, without hands or feet, eternal, all-pervading, omnipresent, exceedingly subtle, that is the Undecaying which the wise perceive as the source of beings.
7. As a spider sends forth and draws in (its thread), as herbs grow on the earth, as the hair (grows) on the head and the body of a living person, so from the Imperishable arises here the universe.
8. By contemplative power *Brahman* expands. From that food is produced. From food, life (thence) mind, (thence) the reals (the five elements); (thence) the worlds; (thence the rituals) in the rituals, immortality.
9. He who is all-knowing and all-wise, whose austerity consists of knowledge, from him are born this Brahmā (*Hiraṇyagarbha*), name-shape and food.

— *Muṇḍaka Upaniṣad* I.1.6-9; tr. S. Radhakrishnan[2]

III

The following passage describes the fruits of Brahmā-worship, which figures prominently in early Buddhist conceptions of the Hinduism.

1. This is that truth. The works which the sages saw in the hymns are variously spread forth in the three Vedas. Perform them constantly, ye lovers of truth. This is your path to the world of good deeds.

---

2. S. Radhakrishnan, ed., *The Principal Upaniṣads*, pp. 672-74. Radhakrishnan seems to offer an Advaitic interpretation here, see ibid., p. 65.

2. When the flame (which) moves after the fire has been kindled, then one should throw with faith his oblations between the two portions of melted butter.
3. He whose agnihotra sacrifice is not followed by the sacrifice of the new moon and of the full moon, by the four months' sacrifice, by the ritual (performed in the harvest season) is without guests, without oblations, without the ceremony to all the gods or gives offerings contrary to rule, (such conduct) destroys his worlds till the seventh.
4. The seven moving tongues of fire are the black, the terrific, the swift as mind, the very red, the very smoky-coloured, the spark blazing, the all-shaped goddess.
5. Whosoever performs works, makes offerings when these (tongues) are shining and at the proper time, these (offerings) in the form of the rays of the sun lead him to that (world) where the one lord of the gods abides.
6. The radiant offerings invite him with the words, "come, come", and carry the sacrifice by the rays of the sun, honouring him and saluting him with pleasing words: "This is your holy world of Brahmā won through good deeds."

— *Muṇḍaka Upaniṣad* I.2.1-6; tr. S. Radhakrishnan[3]

3. S. Radhakrishnan, ed., *The Principal Upaniṣads*, pp. 674-76.

7

Viṣṇu

I

The *Kaṭha Upaniṣad* is associated with Viṣṇu, in the sense that the successful spiritual aspirant wins the abode of Viṣṇu. The means which lead to this end are described in terms of a metaphor, which was destined to become a prominent feature of Hindu thought. If it is true that the Aryans owed their military success to the use of the chariot, then the transformation of consciousness wrought by its employment in the following passage also calls for celebration.

Parable of the Individual Soul in a Chariot

3. Know thou the soul (*ātman*, self) as riding in a chariot,
The body as the chariot.
Know thou the intellect (*buddhi*) as the chariot-driver,
And the mind (*manas*) as the reins.

4. The senses (*indriya*), they say, are the horses;
The objects of sense, what they range over.
The self combined with senses and mind
Wise men call "the enjoyer" (*bhoktṛ*).

5. He who has not understanding (*a-vijñāna*),
Whose mind is not constantly held firm —
His senses are uncontrolled,
Like the vicious horses of a chariot-driver.

6. He, however, who has understanding,
Whose mind is constantly held firm —
His senses are under control,
Like the good horses of a chariot-driver.

Intelligent Control of the Soul's Chariot Needed to Arrive beyond Reincarnation

7. He, however, who has not understanding,
Who is unmindful and ever impure,
Reaches not the goal,
But goes on to reincarnation (*saṁsāra*).

8. He, however, who has understanding,
Who is mindful and ever pure,
Reaches the goal
From which he is born no more.

9. He, however, who has the understanding
of a chariot-driver,
A man who reins in his mind —
He reaches the end of his journey,
That highest place of Viṣṇu

— *Kaṭha Upaniṣad* I.1.3.1-9; tr. R.E. Hume.[1]

II

The doctrine of *avatāra,* or the periodic incarnationary descent of God in the world to save it from premature dissolution, became closely associated with Viṣṇu. One of its earliest unambiguous formulations occurs in the *Bhagavad-Gītā,* in which Kṛṣṇa, elsewhere identified *as an incarnation* of Viṣṇu, is identified with Viṣṇu as such (XI.24.30). These famous lines are found in the early part of Chapter Four. The text covers the early section. The key verses are 7 and 8 but the ninth is also included, as indicating the salvific force of the knowledge of these incarnations.

1. Robert Ernest Hume, tr., *The Thirteen Principal Upaniṣads,* New York, Oxford University Press, 1968 [1921], pp. 351-52.

Chapter IV

The Blessed One said:

1. This discipline to Vivasvat
   I proclaimed; 'tis eternal:
   Vivasvat told it to Manu,
   Manu spake it to Ikṣvāku.

2. Thus received in line of succession,
   The royal seers knew it.
   In a long course of time in this world this
   Discipline became lost, scorcher of the foe.

3. This very same by Me to thee today,
   This ancient discipline, is proclaimed.
   Thou art My devotee and friend, that is why;
   For this is a supreme secret.

Arjuna Said:

4. Later Thy birth,
   Earlier the birth of Vivasvat:
   How may I understand this,
   That Thou didst proclaim it in the beginning, as Thou sayest?

The Blessed One Said:

5. For Me have passed many
   Births, and for thee, Arjuna;
   These I know all;
   Thou knowest not, scorcher of the foe.

6. Tho unborn, tho My self is eternal,
   Tho Lord of Beings,
   Resorting to My own material nature
   I came into being by My own mysterious power.

7. For whenever of the right
   A languishing appears, son of Bharata,

A rising up of the unright,
Then I send Myself forth.

8. For protection of the good,
And for destruction of evil-doers,
To make a firm footing for the right,
I come into being in age after age.

9. My wondrous birth and actions
Whoso knows thus as they truly are,
On leaving the body, to rebirth
He goes not; to Me he goes, Arjuna

— *Bhagavad-Gītā* IV-1-9; tr. Franklin Edgerton[2]

III

Although Viṣṇu has taken, and, is perhaps even now, taking numerous incarnations, a standard list of ten such incarnations started appearing around 400 CE. Read closely, the *Gītā* verses imply that the more *dharma* degenerates the oftener will Kṛṣṇa incarnate. At least in terms of the standard list, however, this does not seem to be the case and it has been suggested that perhaps "quality counteracts the lack of quantity", in the sense that the *avatāra*s manifest differing degrees of Viṣṇu, a view in accordance with which Kṛṣṇa is a *pūrṇāvatāra* (a full manifestation of Viṣṇu).

One of the more intriguing incarnations of Viṣṇu is that of the dwarf (Vāmana), especially as it results in the undoing of a "righteous demon", of even a good guy.[3] The three strides with which Viṣṇu covers the worlds in this account are reminiscent of his description as Trivikrama in the *Ṛg-Veda*.

2. Franklin Edgerton, *The Bhagavad-Gītā*, Cambridge: Harvard University Press, 1974; first published 1944, pp. 23-24.
3. Clifford Hospital, *The Righteous Demon: A Study of Bali*, Vancouver: University of British Columbia, 1960.

Brahma Purāṇa 73

Nārada spoke:

The goddess who resides in the water jar and who enhances your holiness, how did she come to the land of mortals? Tell me that at length, O Lord.

Brahmā Spoke:

The great *daitya* named Bali, unconquerable enemy of the gods, endowed with *dharma* and honour, protector of the people, devoted to his *guru*, with his truth, strength, and might, with his gifts and tolerance, he cannot be compared in the triple world. Having seen his great prosperity, the worried gods said to each other, "How is Bali winning? He controls the sovereignty of the triple world, free from troubles; no enemies or sickness or anxieties exist at all. There is no drought nor *adharma* nor scarcity nor evil folk; these are not seen even in dreams while Bali is reigning".

The gods, who were torn by the arrows of his prosperity, who were split in two by the sword of his fame, whose bodies were broken by the spear of his authority, could find no refuge. Having first shown jealousy, then they took counsel. Wearied, they went to Viṣṇu, their bodies shining from the fire of his fame.

The gods spoke:

O bearer of the conch, discus, and mace, we are indeed lifeless and suffering. You always bear weapons for our sake. O World Protector, even when you are our protector, we have such suffering. One bows to you, but how does one praise a *daitya*? We seek refuge in you with the mind, with acts, and with words. Having sought refuge at your feet, how could we praise a *daitya*? We worship you with great sacrifices, we speak with praises, O Acyuta, our sole refuge is you; how could we praise a *daitya*? The gods with Indra at their head continually receive their vigour from you, having reached the station granted by you; how could we praise a *daitya*? Having taken the form of Brahmā, you are the creator, having become Viṣṇu, you protect; through the energy of Rudra, you are the destroyer; how could we praise a *daitya*? Sovereignty is the more important thing in the world, but we are deprived of sovereignty; what is the use? Our sovereignty is conquered, O Lord of gods, how can we praise a *daitya*? You have no beginning and are endless, you are the support of the world, the *guru* of the world. How can we praise a *daitya* enemy who is mortal? Having conquered the triple world with vitality, our bodies are well nourished through your sovereignty, we are steadfast, O Lord of gods; how could we praise a *daitya*?

Brahmā spoke:

The destroyer of the *daityas*, having thus heard the speech, spoke to all the immortals about the accomplishment of the purpose of the gods.

The Blessed One spoke:

The Daitya Bali is my devotee, he is inviolable to gods and demons. As you are nourished by me, so is Bali nourished by me. O gods, having seized the sovereignty in Indra's heaven without a battle, having bound Bali and having spoken the *mantra*, I will give you the sovereignty.

Brahmā spoke:

Having thus spoken, the host of gods went to the heaven, and the Blessed One, Lord of gods, entered Aditi's womb. When he was born there were festivals; he was born a brāhmaṇa dwarf, lord of sacrifice, the sacrificial *puruṣa*.

Meanwhile, O Excellent brāhmaṇa, mighty Bali prepared for the horse-sacrifice, joined by the best of *ṛṣis* as the sacrificing priests, gods, *gandharvas*, and *nāgas* were also present for the sake of a share of the offering. "May it be given, may it be eaten, and may there be worship", one by one and again and again, and "that is enough", while such speeches were going on, quietly Vāmana approached that place, chanting a *Sāma* verse. Vāmana, with colourful rings, approached the sacrificial enclosure, praising that sacrifice. The Bhārgava, having seen the dwarf god, destroyer of *daityas*, bearing the form of a brāhmaṇa, having quickly recognised him as the donor of the fruit of sacrifice and asceticism, he hurriedly spoke to the king of great splendour, to mighty Bali, who is a conqueror by *kṣātradharma*, a giver of wealth through devotion, consecrated in the sacrifice with his wife, O Excellent One. Meditating on the sacrificial *puruṣa*, and making the oblation separately, wise Śukra, that tiger among Bhṛgus, spoke to him.

Śukra spoke:

He who has arrived at your sacrifice, the brāhmaṇa bearing the form of a dwarf, is not a brāhmaṇa, O Bali; truly he is the lord of the sacrifice, the bearer of the sacrifice. Indeed, this "child" has arrived to beg you for the welfare of the gods. Having consulted with me, O Lord, afterwards you should grant.

Brahmā spoke:

Then Bali, conqueror of foes, spoke to his chief priest, the Bhārgava. "I am fortunate; the lord of sacrifice incarnate comes to my home. He comes and asks for something; what advice remains?"

Brahmā spoke:

Having thus spoken with his chief priest Śukra, he went with his wife to where the chief of brāhmaṇas, Vāmana, son of Aditi, was. Having joined his hands together in a reverent gesture, he said to him, "please say whatever you like". Then Vāmana said, "O chief of kings, give three steps of land;

nothing can be accomplished with wealth". But then, saying yes to him, and letting the water go from the pitcher that was adorned with various jewels, when the chief priest Śukra and the head *ṛṣi*s saw this, while the world guardians and the assembly of *daitya*s were watching, and when the shout of victory was sounded, he gave the land to Vāmana.

Slowly Vāmana spoke, "Salutations, O Prosperous King! Give me land measuring three steps so that I can go quickly". The *daitya* lord spoke as he watched Vāmana. The Lord of sacrifice, sacrificial *puruṣa*, endless Acyuta, the god striding widely, bearer of the step grew until the moon and sun were in the middle of his breasts. Having seen him, the *daitya* king, together with his wife, spoke modestly. "O Viṣṇu, Lord of the world, stride as far as possible, Container of the Whole World, O Lord of gods, now my devotion is victorious, O Creator of all things".

Brahmā spoke:

Simultaneously, Viṣṇu, the Lord of great sacrifice, spoke these words: "O Lord of *daitya*s, Long-armed one, I will stride: Watch, O Daitya Chief".

Brahmā spoke:

Thus speaking, Bali said, "Stride, O Viṣṇu, again and again". Having set down his foot on the tortoise shell, he planted his foot at the sacrifice of Bali. The second step reached the eternal Brahmaloka.

Bali said:

The whole world was created by *you*, O Lord of gods, I am not the creator. By your fault it became small; what can I do, O World Receptacle? I have never said a false word before, O Keśava; my words are truthful. Place your foot on my back.

Brahmā spoke:

Then pleased, the Blessed One having the threefold form spoke, honoured by the gods. "Choose a boon, God bless you, O *daitya king*. I am pleased by your devotion!"

Brahmā spoke:

He said to the world protector, "I do not beg you with your three steps". Viṣṇu, pleased, gave what he himself desired in his mind. Hari gave him sovereignty of *rasātala* and, in the future, the abode of Indra again, sovereignty of his own soul, and indestructible glory. Thus, having given all this to Bali, Hari established Bali, enemy of the gods, in *rasātala*, together with his children and accompanied by his wives. He gave the sovereignty of the gods to Śatakratu according to his birth, and that abode which is worshipped by the gods. O Great sage, Viṣṇu, having reached my house, the second step of my father, having seen that abode, I thought: "What shall I do that will be auspicious when the step of Viṣṇu arrives?" Looking all around and thinking my jar might be the best, that holiest water which was given by Śiva, chosen as the best, grants wishes, supreme, and causes peace, auspicious and yields auspiciousness eternally, grants enjoyment and freedom, like one's own mother, elixir of the worlds, healing and pure, holy, purifying, worthy of worship, most excellent and eminent, endowed with qualities, purifying the worlds by its recollection, how much more from its sight? "Having become pure, I will use such water as an offering to my father". Having thought this, and taking that water, it was used as an offering. That offering of water fell with incantations on the foot of Viṣṇu. The water, having fallen on Meru, reached the earth in four parts, on the east, south, west, and north. That water which fell on the south side, O Muni, Śaṅkara seized it with his matted locks. And that which fell on the west side, went into the water jar. And that which fell on the north side,

Viṣṇu seized that water. And on the east side, the gods, manes, and world guardians seized that good water; and that is why it is considered superior. The waters that are the mothers of the world and that fell on the south side, they are born from the foot of Viṣṇu, and they are the mothers of the world, worthy of praise. They reside in the matted locks of Śiva and make themselves manifest at an auspicious time. And one shall obtain all desires by remembering their power.

— Tr. Deborah A. Soifer[4]

IV

Our sense of devotional appreciation may now be enhanced with an elegantly brief hymn in praise of Viṣṇu attributed to Śaṅkara.

O Lord, even after realising that there is no real difference between the individual soul and *Brahman,* I beg to state that I am yours and that you are mine. The wave belongs to the ocean and not the ocean to the wave.[5]

V

In this final section we include an account of an encounter between a traditional Vaiṣṇava (a devotee of Viṣṇu) and a modern scholar of religion. It relates to Kṛṣṇa, one of the two most popular incarnations in which Viṣṇu is worshipped (the other being that of Rāma). The occasion is the birth anniversary of Kṛṣṇa. The place: Vṛndāvana.

> "Tell me about the birth of God as Jesus Christ", Gopalji begged of me. "Let me understand Jesus the way you understand him, let me see his heart".

---

4. Deborah A. Soifer, *The Myths of Narasiṁha and Vāmana: Two Avatārs in Cosmological Perspective* Albany, N.Y.: State University of New York Press, 1991, pp. 194-99.
5. S. Radhakrishnan, tr., op. cit., p. 38.

He gave me the gospels — he read them daily. "In those days it came to pass that the emperor Augustus issued an edict. . . ". In his mind, Gopalji had often contemplated the scene — Joseph and Mary and the child, the shepherd and the entire landscape. With folded hands he said: "Peace to God on high and on earth peace among men. . . *oṁ, śānti, oṁ*". He knew the texts by heart.

I began to tell him what Christmas meant for those of us who grew up as Christians. The festive midnight services, the stars and bells, the Christmas tree and the lights. I told him of all the Christmas celebrations I could remember. Of the children who wait for little Jesus and are happy about the toys, cakes and candles. I told him of Christmas in wartime, the Holy Night in the air raid shelter, of Christmas during the evacuation, of Christmas in the forest with the boy scouts, of the secret preparing and buying of gifts in order to make someone happy, of the rich man's Christmas and Christmas of the poor. I told him about Christmas in Munich and the "Christkindlmarkt", the Christmas bazaar, of Christmas in Rome, with the shepherds from the Abruzzi mountains playing their bagpipes, of Christmas in Vienna with the large choirs and orchestras in the churches, of Christmas in Bombay with balloons and paper garlands and the five-pronged stars wishing everyone a "Merry Xmas", of Christmas in Mathura and the youngmen from Bihar who, after midnight service, danced their folk-dances around the church the whole night through. I tried to make him feel how, each year, the enchantment of Christmas makes people kinder and more helpful, how the memory of God becoming man makes people grow more human, how it reveals their goodwill and their kind heart, how Christ has the power, even today, to move hearts.

Gopalji listened with interest. "The Lord comes for the delight of the good. The wicked ones do not even see Him. He is mysterious — he wants to serve us and to be served by us. He wants to be our child and friend and playmate and husband. He wants to jest with us and play, like a small child. . . ". He laughed aloud. On the road we could see a man shouting and abusing. With one hand he held his head, with the other one he tried to retrieve the end of his turban which was dangling high above him. A little monkey, the kind that hop around by the hundreds here in town, had grabbed the headgear of the villager with a daring sweep. With both hands he pulled it. Half a dozen little Hanumāns watched with interest. The smallest ones clung to their mothers. "God has a very good sense of humour", said Gopalji, still laughing. "Jestingly, he wants to rid us of all that is superfluous". The man with the turban was still scolding; without his turban. Half a dozen monkeys amused themselves with the long bright red strip of cloth, they wrapped themselves in it, rolled one another about and screeched with delight. Lastly, they let it flutter from a branch. "Would the silly man quarrel with the monkey if he thought that Kṛṣṇa was wanting to play with his turban?" Gopalji interjected. "Everything is a play, his *līlā*. If only people could see that he is in everything, that everything proceeds from him, sickness and health, life and death, the turban and the monkey — would they still grieve or get agitated? People do not recognise him, although he is everywhere. They are misled by their own covetousness. But why talk about it? Let us meditate on the mystery of the birth of the Unborn, who is born in many forms".

"In the beginning was the Word, and Word was with God, and God was the Word. . . ".

"Oṁ. . .", said Gopalji. "He is the mysterious *mantra*, the word existing from eternity, the name of God who was given to men, as the safest means for crossing the ocean of this transitoriness. In God's name is all power and grace — He purifies us. . . ".

Gopalji listened carefully when I told him of the eternal birth of the Son from the Father. That, too, was not new to him.

"*Rāma nāma satya hai, Rāma nāma satya hai. . .*" — it came upon us in a monotonous rhythm. One of the many processions to the burning ghats. "*Rāma nāma satya hai. . .* ". It faded into the distance.

"Do you think we will be together in eternity?" Gopalji asked me. "Would you consider me a Christian, as I am?"

"Love God, with all your heart and with all your power and your neighbour, as yourself", Christ had replied to one who wanted to know the meaning of "Christianity". Gopalji loved God in the way he understood him — he employed all his time and strength to serve him, to know him better. Every instant his name was on his lips; ceaselessly the *mālā*, a kind of rosary, moved through his fingers — each bead an invocation of the name of God. He was good to all who came to him. He possessed nothing beyond the few trifles in this room. He tried to incorporate the teachings of his Mahāprabhu, his "Great Lord" — to be humbler than a blade of grass, more patient than a tree, and to praise God always. On many a day he fasted completely. He had no enemy. "I am the door", Christ had said: "all who came before me were thieves and robbers". Was the one who had taught him to regard everything as *līlā*, as the play of a loving God, a thief and a robber? I wonder if he did not venerate Christ in Kr̥ṣṇa — and Kr̥ṣṇa within Christ? Was he not closer to the mystery of God and his incarnation than many who call themselves Christians? Was it not Christ who united us in friendship, who had brought us together here on Kr̥ṣṇa's birthday to speak of his birth?

What does it mean to be a Christian? We have a small verse from one of our poet-mystics: "And if Christ was born a thousand times in Bethlehem and not within you, you would be lost eternally." Christ must be born in each one of us. Gopalji was already "reborn", a *dvijāti* — he had received the *saṁnyāsī*'s initiation, was dead to the world. What more was necessary?

Would he see Christ in the flesh as God, if he were baptised? No — it was a matter of other depths: faith, communion with God, love.

"Gopalji," I asked. "Have you ever doubted Kṛṣṇa?"

"Yes," he replied. "As a young man I have doubted. I found everything so childish and unscientific and boring. But my *gurujī*, my religious teacher, opened my eyes to reality. And since then, I have never again doubted God — only men and the world. I have begun to understand that he is reality, that our so-called science remains on the surface, that he lives in the innermost of our heart, where no human science penetrates. It is because of grace that we recognise him. Doubt is the worst kind of poison for the man who seeks God. He must believe, believe with all his heart, even if all the other people take him for a madman, just as they thought of Caitanya and Mīrā Bāī and Ramakrishna — those great saints — just mad. They were not insane — the world was insane. They were within reality, the world is unreal. God is everywhere, but men are blind."

"Gopalji," I asked. "Is it not presumptuous to choose one's own *iṣṭadevatā*, the God one adores?"

"It is not we who choose our God, it is God who chooses us", he replied. "It is in his power to attract or repel us, to let us do good or evil. We cannot do anything on our own. But even when he destroys us, it is for our salvation, if we only see that it is He. But human beings forget so easily. Today they celebrate his birth — tomorrow they have forgotten him. Sometimes I am so filled with nausea that I call for him with tears in my eyes."

"Is he not continuously arriving?" I interjected. "Even in the people of goodwill who proclaim his peace? He has told us to proclaim his kingdom — to live in expectation of his arrival. He is still being born out of God and within human beings who welcome the word of God."

"Yes," said Gopalji, "he is still being born." For a long while he contemplated the child Kṛṣṇa and hummed a little *bhajana* to himself. "Yes, there are good people even today; but they are not the loud ones who speak over the wireless, not the famous ones, who have ministers taking part on their pious *kīrtana* singing. They are the quiet and the patient ones — they are the salt of the earth. God visits them and in them He comes to us. Do you know the story of Daridra Nārāyaṇa? God took on the shape of a poor man. He went to the richest man in the village and asked for food and shelter for the night. But that one chased him away. He went to the poorest man who lived outside the village. This one welcomed him honourably and shared his poor meal and his miserable hut with him. When God asked what reward he wished to have, he replied that he wished to serve God. Has not God been born within the poor man?"

It was still *Janmāṣṭamī*, Kṛṣṇa's birthday. On a pony cart, the festively attired boys passed by with solemn demeanour. They would, in the evening, perform the *rāsalīlā*, the play of Kṛṣṇa with the *gopīs*; the play of God with humankind, . . . and fulfilment of human life. Gopalji wanted to know whether we, too, played God's *līlā* during Christmas. Yes, we, too, play God's *līlā* — with flutes and violins and choirs, in the paintings and sculptures of great masters, in the fervent representations of folk art. India already has her Indian Christmas plays — her Christmas songs and dances expressing the joy over his arrival. "The joy over his arrival", Gopalji repeated pensively. "Is it not the only real joy we have? Everything is transitory — everything dies. Only he does not die and those who know him. I do not long for riches or fame — I only long for him. Master Nārada, the author of the Bhakti-sūtras, says that the love a lover feels when he is separated from his loved one is the highest kind of love. Sometimes, I think I am unable to bear the pain of separation any longer. Perhaps, we have to sink even deeper into ignorance, to come away from him even further, feel the pain of separation even more sharply, before he comes."

Gopalji was silent. For minutes, not a word was said. But we both know that we were thinking of the same thing: of him and of him coming.

And when he comes, what will be? Will men recognise him this time and accept him? Will they really love him? Will he not, once again, shame the wisdom of the scribes, once again upset the tables of moneychangers in the temple, once again disappoint the hopes of the politicians? Will he not again be crucified and buried — and forgotten?

"He has come", said Gopalji. "We must look for him, He only hides so that our impatience may grow and our love be purified — that we do not seek our pleasure, but his. He does not come to ease our life on earth — he comes out of his divine will, to teach us his love."

A neighbour dropped in. He seated himself near us. A few more arrived. It was time for the daily *bhajana*. I left Gopalji and went home. The peacocks complained again. The frogs quacked contentedly in the large puddles created by the rain. The vultures sat peevishly and watchfully on their tree. They were awaiting daylight.

I began with Mass. Alone, in my poor room. The bells pealed from the nearby temple, bells rung by the people as they enter the temple. From nearby houses, I could hear the *bhajana*s, the rolling *ḍhola*s and the jingling of bells. Pilgrims passed by my window — "*Hare Kṛṣṇa, Kṛṣṇa Hare. . .*" Introit, Kyrie — the temple bells mixed with the Gloria. The prayer was accompanied by the *kīrtana*. And the gospel told of the transfiguration of the Lord — "do not tell anyone of it before the Son of the man has risen from the dead". Gopalji was in my mind; he would be speaking now in front of his small community about the advent of God, his advent in Gokula and in Bethlehem, in the hearts of men. He would try to interpret to his friends the mystery of the eternal birth of the Word from the Father — and again he would be so moved as to burst into sobs and tears, because he could not bear it that he was unable to see the Lord. Did I not also offer his pain and his longing on the paten? Was the wine not also the expression of his love? And did not Christ also transform Gopalji's miserable humanness into his own humanity, into his love for the Father? Would he not also take part in my communion with Him?

It was August 6, 1963 — but no Christmas has made me understand better the mystery of the coming of God, no Christmas has awakened within me a more urgent longing. And no Christmas will pass without the presence, in my mind, of Gopalji, of his love for his Lord, his longing, his question. Nor shall I forget the peacocks, the frogs, the monkeys and the vultures, nor the lightning and the rushing of water. But more than anything else I shall carry this with me as my Christmas mystery: that God gives to a man so much longing for his coming.

— Klaus K. Klostermaier.[6]

6. Klaus K. Klostermaier, *Hindu and Christian in Vrindaban*, London: SLM Press Ltd., 1969, pp. 80-87, diacritics added.

8

Śiva

I

The *Śvetāśvatara Upaniṣad* marks the culmination of the creedal development of Rudra-Śiva."The beginnings of the conception can be traced back to the early hymns, where we find Rudra as the personification of the destructive powers of nature as exemplified, for instance in storms and lightning. Indeed, the name Rudra literally means 'howler'. The hymns devoted to him in the *R̥g-Veda* are only a very few; but some of the features, predominantly associated with Śiva in later times, are already found mentioned in them, such as his dwelling in the mountains, his having braided hair and his wearing a hide. In later stages he comes to be represented as the patron as well as the pattern of ascetics. On account of his generally terrific character, he was invoked in those early times in order that he might become auspicious or *śiva*. This name of '*Śiva*' becomes his distinctive designation in the later portions of the Veda. He also comes there to be described as the great God (*mahādeva*). In the Śvetāśvatara Upaniṣad (in which the conception blends now and then with that of The Absolute), he holds the same conspicuous position. . . ."[1]

1. He is the One who, spreading wide his net,
   Rules with his sovereign powers:
   By his sovereign powers these worlds He rules.
   He is One [and One abides],

---

1. M. Hiriyanna, *The Essentials of Indian Philosophy*, London, George Allens & Unwin, 1968, p. 33.

As [others] come to be and grow together.
Whoso knows this becomes immortal.

2. For One is Rudra — they stand not for a second —
Who all the worlds doth rule by his sovereign powers:
Over against [his] creatures stands He, protector;
All worlds He emanated,
[All worlds] will He roll up at the end of time.

3 His eyes on every side, on every side his face,
On every side his arms, his feet on every side:
With arms and wings He together forges
Heaven and earth, begetting them, [He,] God, the One!

4. He, of gods the source and origin,
All-sovereign Rudra, mighty Seer
Of old begat the Golden Embryo:
May He conjoin us with a lucid mind (*buddhi*)!

5. Dweller in the mountains, Thyself reveal to us
In thy fairest form (*tanu*), [great] Rudra,
In a form auspicious (*śiva*), [a form] not cruel,
[A form] that displays no evil!

6. Dweller in the mountains, make thine arrow kind (Śiva),
[The arrow] Thou carriest in thy hand to shoot it:
Protector of the mountains, do not hurt
To man or beast.

7. Higher than this, than *Brahman* higher, the mighty [God],
Hidden in all beings, in each according to his kind,
The One, all things encompassing, the Lord —
By knowing Him a man becomes immortal.

8. I know that mighty Person,
Sun-coloured beyond the darkness:
By knowing Him indeed a man surpasses death;
No other path is there on which to go.

9. Beyond Him is nothing whatsoever, no other thing;
No one is more minute than He, no one more vast:
Like a sturdy tree firm-fixed in heaven He stands,
The One, the Person, this whole universe full filling!

10. Than this yet more exalted
Is That which has no form, no imperfection:
Whoso knows this becomes immortal,
The rest must suffer misery.

11. The face, the head, the neck of all is He,
In the heart of every being He makes his home,
All things pervading, Blessed Lord (Bhagavat);
Hence is [He called] "Benign" Śiva, penetrating everywhere.

— *Śvetāśvatara Upaniṣad* III.1-11; tr. R.C. Zaehner.[2]

II

The *liṅga* is the symbol of Śiva *par excellence*. In place of citing from original texts we have chosen a modern expository piece as more likely to promote a deeper understanding of the multivalent symbol:

Rudra's birth from Prajāpati took place in the former aeon. In a subsequent aeon, Rudra/Śiva was born from Brahmā the Creator, unsuccessful in creating human beings. He was born from the angry frown of the Creator's forehead. Śiva was charged by his father to create mortals. Śiva, however, refused to create fallible, imperfect beings. He responded to Brahmā's command by castrating himself. He tore of his phallus (*liṅga*); it sunk into the ground. Or, according to another tradition, when commanded by Brahmā to create mortals, Śiva turned into a post (*sthāṇu*). The severed *liṅga* of Śiva, fallen to the ground, penetrated the netherworld and shot up

2. R.C. Zaehner, tr., *Hindu Scriptures*, New York, Dutton Everyman's Library, 1966, pp. 207-09.

into the empyrean, a burning pillar of flames. Myth tells of its transcosmic dimension.

The two alternative myths, the one of Śiva turning into a post, the other of his self-castration, have their equivalents in the visual form of the *liṅga*. The *liṅga*, a bivalent aniconic symbol in shape and meaning, marks the presence of the invisible, transcendental reality of Śiva. The word *liṅga* means "sign", and particularly, the male sign of sex, the phallus. The solid, concrete shape of the *liṅga* occupies the central position in the worship of Śiva. Set up on earth, a *liṅga* whether made of stone, wood, or metal, is post-or pillar-shaped. Its earliest examples show its pillar shape to be in the likeness of a phallus; significantly, one face, or four faces, may project from its shaft. Some of the earliest *liṅga*s are also combined with an anthropomorphic image of Śiva standing in front of it, about equal in height, or even smaller. Or, the *liṅga* may be covered in its entirety with images facing the four directions, a lighthouse for the manifestations of the deity. In a temple of Śiva, the *liṅga* occupies the centre of the innermost sanctuary (*garbhagṛha*). There is no object in the world of Śiva, more sacred than the *liṅga*.

The *liṅga* stands erect (*ūrdhvaliṅga*); its rounded top points upward as if ready to shed seed, yet, by yogic discipline, it is capable of restraining the potent substance. The meaning of the *ūrdhvaliṅga* is ambivalent, and its shape made by art is a symbol of potency and of its control. It is the *liṅga* of Śiva the Ascetic, full of the seeds of all life to be, withheld by yogic discipline, so as not to be spent but to ascend within the body, with which anthropomorphic imagination endows Śiva, the Great Yogī.

Śiva is the great ascetic god, the Great Yogī, Lord of Yogīs, teacher of Yoga, the ancient discipline practised in the days of the Haṛappā Civilization (third millennium BCE). Carved on some of its diminutive reliefs is a main figure in Yoga posture, unmistakable in the most elaborate of these anthropomorphic representations. The discipline of yoga is practiced to one end: self-mastery that comprises mind and body and readies the living being for the realisation of ultimate reality. The striving for ultimate reality guided by yoga is carried out within the living being and entails the control of the breath, a control that frees the yogi from worldly attachments and concerns of the "ego". The control, not the rejection, of the passionate self — comprising sex — is the function of yoga.

The power of giving life and also of withholding and transmitting the substance of life into consciousness inheres in the *liṅga*, the sign of Śiva. The ascent of the seed (*ūrdhvaretas*) is indicated by the *liṅga* pointed upward. The transmutation of sexual into mental power, the transubstantiation or the ascent from the earthly plane of sentiency into transcendency, is contained within the symbol of the *liṅga*. This, however, is only one aspect of its significance, seen from the position of the practising yogi. The other aspect of the *liṅga* is ontological.

The concrete shape of the Śiva *liṅga*, of stone, wood, metal, sand, or clay, is understood to be a concretization of subtler stuff, of light or sound — of a light stronger than eyes can see, of a sound in which reverberates the primordial stress of creation. Light and sound are manifestations of movement. It was in a Liṅga of Flames that Śiva was seen by the gods in a cosmic night between the destruction of one universe and the creation of another.

The *liṅga* is also looked upon as the visible form of mantra, that is, of sound before it has become word, of sound forms and of words. The ontology of the cosmos together with that of man's mind and body inheres in the concrete shape of the Śiva *liṅga*. Descending from its apex in the four directions of space to its bottom, the *liṅga*, in a complex system of analogical categories, is understood symbolically as the embodiment of the five elements (ether or space, air, fire, water, and earth), the five sense data (sound, touch, form, taste, and smell), and the five sense faculties (hearing, feeling, seeing, tasting, and smelling). Analogous to the categories of the physical world and of sentiency, higher categories comprising mentation and transcendency have, in ontological order, their symbol in the *liṅga*, the principles of essence (*puruṣa*) and substance (*prakṛti*), universal intellect (*buddhi*), personality (*ahaṁkāra*), and mind (*manas*). Of these and further categories comprising the entire realms of existence and transcendence, the *liṅga* is the pivot.

These sets of categories and others, each comprising five constituents, hinge on the five mantras of Śiva. Each of these mantras evokes in its sound an aspect of the total reality, that of Śiva. Each mantra is represented as a face of Śiva. They emerge and project from the *liṅga* pillar; they are aspects of the divine countenance. Four of the faces look into the four directions of space; as a rule, the fifth face on the top of the *liṅga* — symbolically in transcendence — is invisible. It is not even necessary that all four faces be carved; many *liṅga*s have but one face which implies the others. The five mantras of Śiva precede by centuries the earliest five-faced *liṅga* (*pañcamukhaliṅga*).

The propinquity in a *mukhaliṅga* ("face *liṅga*") of face and *liṅga*, a seemingly startling juxtaposition, is the compacted symbol of the beginning and the end of the ascent of the seed and its transubstantiation in the "subtle body" of the yogi from the basic station of consciousness or centre of realisation (*cakra*) at the root centre (*mūlādhāra*) at the base of the spine, to the highest *cakra* at the *brahmarandhra* on the top of the head. The alchemy within the "subtle body" of the yogi has its synoptic image in the juxtaposition of face and *liṅga* in one sculptural shape. The *mukhaliṅga* presupposes Yoga practice and realisation, and depicts in one image its beginning and end. The method of unilocal or synchronous precipitation of several phases of a process or narrative in one picture is common knowledge in Indian art, as it is in early Christian art and elsewhere.

In the world of Śiva, the significance of the *liṅga* is comparable to that of the Cross in the Christian world, and that of Śiva with the *liṅga*, or of the faces of Śiva together with the shape of the *liṅga*, to the figure of the Saviour on the Cross. The essential myths of the *liṅga* are those of the ascetic god who, at the command of Brahmā to procreate, castrates himself or becomes a post (*sthāṇu*). The castration myth, a sequel to the Wild God's shot in the primordial morning (at Prajāpati), is a myth of self-retaliation; the branchless post in the second myth is a visual confirmation of the first myth.

— Stella Kramrisch[3]

3. Stella Kramrisch, *Manifestations of Shiva*, Philadelphia Museum of Art, 1981, pp. xv-xvi.

9

Jīva

In the two passages on the *jīva*, the first focuses on the distinction between the transmigrating self and the real self — the word *ātman* being used for the self in both the cases, but in the former sense with a prefix.

The second passage states the doctrine of the five sheaths of the human personality as found in the text itself.

I

(*Ātman* by itself refers to the *ātman*. *Bhūtātman* is the same as *jīvātman*.)

The Great Soul, and the Individual, Suffering, Reincarnating Soul

1. Then they said: "Sir, if thus you describe the greatness of this Soul (*Ātman*), there is still another, different one. Who is he, called soul (*ātman*), who, being overcome by the bright or the dark fruits of action (*karman*), enters a good or an evil womb, so that his course is downward or upward and he wanders around, overcome by the pairs of opposite (*dvandva*)?"

The Soul that is Subject to Elements and Qualities, Confused and Self-Conceited, Suffers and Reincarnates

2. [Then he said:] "There is indeed another, different soul, called 'the elemental soul' (*bhūtātman*) — he who, being overcome by the bright or the dark fruits of action, enters a good or an evil womb so that his

course is downward or upward and he wanders around, overcome by the pairs of opposites.

The further explanation of this is:

The five subtle substances (*tanmātra*) are spoken of by the word 'element' (*bhūta*). Likewise, the five gross elements (*mahābhūta*) are spoken of by the word 'element'. Now, the combination of these is said to be 'the body' (*śarīra*). Now, he, assuredly, indeed, who is said to be in 'the body' is said to be 'the eternal soul'. Now, its immortal soul (*ātman*) is like 'the drop of water on the lotus leaf'.

This [elemental soul], verily, is overcome by Nature's (*prakṛti*) qualities (*guṇa*).

Now, because of being overcome, he goes on to the state of confusedness; because of confusedness, he sees not the blessed Lord (*prabhu*), the causer of action, who stands within oneself (*ātmastha*). Borne along and defiled by the stream of qualities (*guṇa*), unsteady, wavering, bewildered, full of desire, distracted, this one goes on to the state of self-conceit (*abhimānatva*). In thinking 'This is I' and 'That is mine', he binds himself with his self, as does a bird with a snare.

Consequently (*anu*) 'being overcome by the fruits of his action, he enters a good or an evil womb, so that his course is downward or upward and he wanders around, overcome by the pairs of opposites'."

"Which one is this?"

Then he said to them:

The Inner Person Remains Unaffected in the Elemental Soul's Transformations

3. "Now, it has elsewhere been said: 'Verily, he who is the doer is the elemental soul. The causer of action through the organs is the inner Person. Now, verily,

as a lump of iron, overcome by fire and beaten by workmen, passes over into a different form — so, assuredly, indeed, the elemental soul, overcome by the inner person and beaten by qualities, passes over into a different form. The mode of that different form, verily, has a fourfold covering, is fourteenfold, is transformed in eighty-four different ways, is a host of beings. These varieties, verily, are driven by the Person, like "the wheel by the potter". Now, as, when a lump of iron is being hammered, the fire [in it] is not overcome, so that person is not overcome. This elemental soul (*bhūtātman*) is overcome (*abhibhūta*) because of its attachment [to Qualities.]"

— *Maitrī Upaniṣad* III.1-3; tr. R.E. Hume[1]

II

The following is the root-text of the doctrine of the five sheaths. The key statements are underlined — the rest consists of elaboration and glorification.

FIRST ANUVĀKA

This, verily, is the person that consists of the essence of food. This, indeed, is his head; this, the right side; this, the left side; this, the body (*ātman*); this, the lower part, the foundation.

As to that there is also this verse:

---

1. Robert Ernest Hume, tr., *The Thirteen Principal Upanishads*, pp. 417-19. The expressions "fourfold", "fourteenfold" and "eighty-four" are to be understood as follows. "Fourfold" may refer "to the doctrine of the four sheaths (*kośa*), namely food, breath, mind, and knowledge or, according to the scholiast, to the four forms of animal life, characterised as born alive, born from an egg, born from moisture, and born from a germ" (*Ait.* 5.3). "Fourteenfold" may be read as referring "to the fourteen classes of being, *Sāṁkhya-kārikā* 53, or to the fourteen worlds of *Vedāntasāra* 12.9 — so Deussen interprets" (ibid., p. 419).

SECOND ANUVĀKA

Food the Supporting, yet Consuming, Substance of all Life; a Phase of Brahma

From food, verily, creatures are produced
Whatsoever [creatures] dwell on earth.
Moreover by food, in truth, they live.
Moreover into it also they finally pass.
For truly, food is the chief of beings;
Therefore it is called a panacea.
Verily, they obtain all food
Who worship Brahma as food.
For truly, food is the chief of beings;
Therefore it is called a panacea.
From food created things are born.
By food, when born, do they grow up.
It both is eaten and eats things.
Because of that it is called food.

The Person Consisting of Breath

Verily, other than and within that one that consists of the essence of food is the self that consists of breath. By that this is filled. This, verily, has the form of a person. According to that one's personal form is the one with the form of a person. The in-breath (*prāṇa*) is its head; the diffused breath (*vyāna*), the right wing; the out-breath (*apāna*), the left wing; space, the body (*ātman*); the earth, the lower part, the foundation.

As to that there is also this verse:

THIRD ANUVĀKA

Breath, The Life of All Living Beings; A Phase of Brahma

The gods do breathe along with breath (*prāṇa*),
As also men and beasts.
For truly, breath is the life (*āyus*) of beings
Therefore it is called the Life-of-all (*sarvāyuṣa*).
To a full life (*sarvam āyus*) go they
Who worship Brahma as breath.
For truly, breath is the life of beings;
Therefore, it is called the Life-of-all.

This, indeed, is its bodily self (*śarīra-ātman*), as of the former.

The Person Consisting of Mind

Verily, other that and within that one that consists of breath is a self that consists of mind (*manomaya*). By that this is filled. This, verily, has the form of a person. According to that one's personal form is this one with the form of a person. The Yajur-Veda is its head; the Rig-Veda, the right side; the Sama-Veda, the left side; teaching, the body (*ātman*); the Hymns of the Atharvanas and Aṅgirases, the lower part, the foundation.

As to that there is also this verse:

FOURTH ANUVĀKA

Inexpressible, fearless bliss; a phase of Brahma

Wherefrom words turn back,
Together with the mind, not having attained —
The bliss of Brahma he who knows,
Fears not at any time at all.

This, indeed, is its bodily self (*śarīra-ātman*), as of the former.

The person consisting of understanding

Verily, other than and within that one that consists of mind is a self that consists of understanding (*vijñānamaya*). By that this is filled. This, verily, has the form of a person. According to that one's personal form is this one with the form of a person. Faith (*śraddhā*) is its head; the right (*ṛta*), the right side; the true (*satya*), the left side; contemplation (*yoga*), the body (*ātman*); might (*mahas*), the lower part, the foundation.

As to that there is also this verse:

FIFTH ANUVĀKA

Understanding, all-directing; a saving and satisfying phase of Brahma

Understanding directs the sacrifice;
And deeds also it directs.
'Tis understanding that all the gods
Do worship as Brahma, as chief.
If one knows Brahma as understanding,
And if he is not heedless thereto,
He leaves his sins (*pāpman*) in the body
And attains all desires.

This, indeed, is its bodily self, as of the former.

The person consisting of bliss

Verily, other than and within that one that consists of understanding is a self that consists of bliss (*ānandamaya*). By that this is filled. That one, verily, has the form of a person. . . .

— *Taittirīya Upaniṣad* II.1-5; tr. R.E. Hume[2]

2. Robert Ernest Hume, tr., op. cit., pp. 283-86.

10

Saṁsāra

The concept of *saṁsāra*, often translated as metempsychosis, is a standard feature of classical Hinduism. "The conditions under which reincarnation takes place, and which are often picturesquely described, involve an explicit relationship between the fault committed and the condition imposed, as a result — sometimes on the basis of a childish symbolism or even a pun, a stealer of oil being reborn as a scurf (because another name for scurf is 'oil-drinker'), whereas, a jewel thief has the luck to be reborn as a goldsmith. In the systematic expositions that occur in the later literature the scheme is as follows: the soul will be granted a human body after undergoing 84 lakh of preliminary reincarnations; 20 lakh as a plant, 9 as an aquatic creature, 11 as an insect, 10 as a bird, 30 as some kind of cattle, 4 as a monkey; it must then undergo 2 lakh of rebirths in the various estates of man, from the lowest to the highest, before it is liberated from *saṁsāra*."[1]

The word *saṁsāra* appears as such for the first time in the Upaniṣads: in *Kaṭha* III.7; *Śvetāśvatara* VI.16; *Maitrī* VI.28, etc. Each occurrence is significant in its own way.

I

In *Kaṭha Upaniṣad*, a contrast is drawn between those who "go on" to rebirths, which is *saṁsāra*, and those who do not.

> He, however, who has no understanding,
> Who is unmindful and even impure,

1. Louis Renou, *The Nature of Hinduism* (tr. Patrick Evans), New York: Walker and Company, 1951, p. 67

Reaches not the goal,
But goes on to reincarnation (*saṁsāra*).
He, however, who has understanding,
Who is mindful and ever pure,
Reaches the goal,
From which he is born no more — III.7-8[2]

[How one might fare in *saṁsāra* is also explained.]

Some go into a womb
For the embodiment of a corporeal being,
Others go into a stationary thing
According to their deeds (*karman*)
According to their knowledge. — V.7[3]

II

In the *Śvetāśvatara Upaniṣad*, as in the *Kaṭha*, it is the contrast between *saṁsāra*, and freedom from it, which is emphasised. What gives this citation its unique flavour is the association of the doctrine with God, a connection not always insisted upon within the tradition.

He who is the maker of all, the all-knower, self-sourced,

Intelligent, the author of time, possessor of qualities, omniscient,

Is the ruler of primary matter (*pradhāna*) and of the spirit (*kṣetrajña*), the lord of qualities (*guṇa*),

The cause of reincarnation (*saṁsāra*) and of liberation (*mokṣa*), of continuance and of bondage. — VI.16[4]

---

2. R.E. Hume, tr., *The Thirteen Principal Upanishads*, London: Oxford University Press, 1968 (1921), p. 352.
3. Ibid., p. 357.
4. Ibid., p. 410.

III

The references in the *Maitrī* are interesting because they make the context of *saṁsāra* both more concrete and more subtle. Whereas the other Upaniṣads merely refer to it as an ongoing process to be brought to an end, *Maitrī* packs more metaphorical punch into its description.

> Henceforth, having seen [the soul] which abides in his own greatness, he looks down upon the wheel of transmigrating existence (*saṁsāra*) as upon a rolling chariot wheel. — VI.28[5]

However, the concept is also subtilised.

> *Saṁsāra* is just one's own thought;
> With effort he should cleanse it, then.
> What is one's thought, that he becomes;
> This is the eternal mystery.
>
> For by tranquillity (*prasāda*) of thought,
> Deeds (*karman*), good and evil, one destroys.
> With soul serene, stayed on the Soul,
> Delight eternal one enjoys! — VI.34[6]

IV

One interpretation of *Kauṣītakī Upaniṣad* I.2 is worth noting. According to this interpretation, the souls of the departed go to the moon. The moon asks the soul, "Who are you?" and if the right answer is not given, the soul returns to the earth in the form of rain[7] and undergoes the following fate:

> But whoever answers it not, him, having become rain, it rains down here. Either as a worm, or as a moth, or as a fish, or as a bird, or as a lion, or as a wild boar, or as a snake, or as

5. R.E. Hume, tr., op. cit., p. 441.
6. Ibid., p. 447.
7. A.L. Basham, *The Origins and Development of Classical Hinduism* (ed. Kenneth G. Zysk), Boston: Beacon Press, 1989, p. 47.

a tiger, or as a person, or as some other in this or that condition, he is born again here according to his deeds (*karman*), according to his knowledge.[8]

"The soul has to choose whether it wishes to return or go on further through the heavenly realms. Appropriate formulas are given, to be pronounced in case of either choice."[9] According to A.L. Basham this is "perhaps the only passage in any Hindu scripture where it is considered that any being would positively wish to be reborn rather than fare onward to complete release from the burden of transmigration."[10]

When he comes thither it asks him:

"Who are you?"

He should reply:

"From the far-shining, O ye seasons, has semen been gathered,

From the fifteenfold produced, from the realm of the fathers.

As such send ye me in a man as an agent.

With a man as an agent in a mother infuse me.

So am I born, being born forth as the twelfth or thirteenth succeeding month, by means of a twelve- or thirteen-folk father. For the knowledge of this was I — for the knowledge of the opposite of this. So bring ye my seasons on to immortality. By this truth, by this austerity I am a season, I am connected with the seasons. Who am I? I am you."

It lets him go further.[11]

---

8. R.E. Hume, tr., op. cit., p. 303.
9. A.L. Basham, op. cit., p. 47.
10. Ibid.
11. R.E. Hume, tr., op. cit., pp. 303-04. The passage is somewhat obscure.

V

For the graphic details of the process of rebirth, which characterises *saṁsāra*, one must turn elsewhere.

1. "O sinless One, the whole sacred law, (applicable) to the four castes, has been declared by thee; communicate to us (now), according to the truth, the ultimate retribution for (their) deeds."
2. To the great sages (who addressed him thus) righteous Bhṛgu, sprung from Manu, answered, "Hear the decision concerning this whole connection with actions."
3. Action, which springs from the mind, from speech, and from the body, produces either good or evil results; by action are caused the (various) conditions of men, the highest, the middling, and the lowest.
4. Know that the mind is the instigator here below, even to that (action) which is connected with the body, (and) which is of three kinds, has three locations, and falls under ten heads.
5. Coveting the property of others, thinking in one's heart of what is undesirable, and adherence to false (doctrines), are the three kinds of (sinful) mental action.
6. Abusing (others, speaking) untruth, detracting from the merits of all men, and talking idly, shall be the four kinds of (evil) verbal action.
7. Taking what has not been given, injuring (creatures) without the sanction of the law, and holding criminal intercourse with another man's wife, are declared to be the three kinds of (wicked) bodily action.
8. (A man) obtains (the result of) a good or evil mental (act) in his mind, (that of) a verbal (act) in his speech, (that of) a bodily (act) in his body.

9. In consequence of (many) sinful acts committed with his body, a man becomes (in the next birth) something inanimate, in consequence (of sins) committed by speech, a bird, or a beast, and in consequence of mental (sins he is reborn in) a low caste.

10. That man is called a (true) *tridaṇḍin* in whose mind these three, the control over his speech (*vāgdaṇḍa*), the control over his thoughts (*manodaṇḍa*), and the control over his body (*kāyadaṇḍa*), are firmly fixed.

11. That man who keeps this threefold control (over himself) with respect to all created beings and wholly subdues desire and wrath, thereby assuredly gains complete success.

12. Him who impels this (corporeal) Self to action, they call the *kṣetrajña* (the knower of the field); but him who does the acts, the wise name *bhūtātman* (the Self consisting of the elements).

13. Another internal Self that is generated with all embodied (*kṣetrajña*s) is called *jīva*, through which (the *kṣetrajña*) becomes sensible of all pleasure and pain in (successive) births.

14. These two, the Great One [usually identified with *jīva*] and the *kṣetrajña*, who are closely united with the elements, pervade him who resides in the multiform created beings.

15. From his body innumerable forms go forth, which constantly impel the multiform creatures to action.

16. Another strong body, formed of particles (of the) five (elements and) destined to suffer the torments (in hell), is produced after death (in the case) of wicked men.

17. When (the evil-doers) by means of that body have suffered there the torments imposed by Yama (its constituent parts) are united, each according to its class,

with those very elements (from which they were taken).

18. He, having suffered for his faults, which are produced by attachment to sensual objects, and which result in misery, approaches, free from stains, those two mighty ones.

19. Those two together examine without tiring the merit and the guilt of that (individual soul), united with which it obtains bliss or misery both in this world and the next.

20. If (the soul) chiefly practised virtue and vice to a small degree, it obtains bliss in heaven, clothed with those very elements.

21. But if it chiefly cleaves to vice and to virtue in a small degree, it suffers, deserted by the elements, the torments inflicted by Yama.

22. The individual soul, having endured those torments of Yama, again enters, free from taint, those very five elements, each in due proportion.

23. Let (man), having recognised even by means of his intellect these transitions of the individual soul (which depend) on merit and demerit, always fix his heart on (the acquisition of) merit.

24. Know goodness (*sattva*), activity (*rajas*), and darkness (*tamas*) to be the three qualities of the Self, with which the Great One always completely pervades all existences.

25. When one of these qualities wholly predominates in a body, then it makes the embodied (soul) eminently distinguished for that quality.

26. Goodness is declared (to have the form of) knowledge, Darkness (of) ignorance, Activity (of) love and hatred; such is the nature of these (three) which is (all-) pervading and clings to everything created.

27. When (man) experiences in his soul a (feeling) full of bliss, a deep calm, as it were, and a pure light, then let him know (that it is) among those three (the quality called) Goodness.

28. What is mixed with pain and does not give satisfaction to the soul one may know (to be the quality of) Activity, which is difficult to conquer, and which ever draws embodied (souls towards sensual objects).

29. What is coupled with delusion, what has the character of an undiscernible mass, what cannot be fathomed by reasoning, what cannot be fully known, one must consider (as the quality of) Darkness.

30. I will, moreover, fully describe the results which arise from these three qualities, the excellent ones, the average ones, and the lowest.

31. The study of the Vedas, austerity, (the pursuit of) knowledge, purity, control over the organs, the performance of meritorious acts and meditation on the Soul, (are) the marks of the quality of Goodness.

32. Delighting in undertakings, want of firmness, commission of sinful acts, and continual indulgence in sensual pleasures, (are) the marks of the quality of Activity.

33. Covetousness, sleepiness, pusillanimity, cruelty, atheism, leading an evil life, a habit of soliciting favours, and inattentiveness, are the marks of the quality of Darkness.

34. Know, moreover, the following to be a brief description of the three qualities, each in its order, as they appear in the three (times, the present, past, and future).

35. When a (man), having done, is doing, or being about to do any act, feels ashamed, the learned may know that all (such acts bear) the mark of the quality of Darkness.

36. But, when (a man) desires (to gain) by an act, much fame in this world and feels no sorrow on failing, know that it (bears the mark of the quality of) Activity.

37. But that (bears) the mark of the quality of Goodness which with his whole (heart) he desires to know, which he is not ashamed to perform, and at which his soul rejoices.

38. The craving after sensual pleasures is declared to be the mark of Darkness, (the pursuit of) wealth (the mark) of Activity (the desire to gain), spiritual merit the mark of Goodness; each later (named quality is) better than the preceding one.

39. I will briefly declare in due order what transmigrations in this whole (world a man) obtains through each of these qualities.

40. Those endowed with Goodness reach the state of gods, those endowed with activity the state of men, and those endowed with darkness for ever sink to the condition of beasts; that is the threefold course of transmigrations.

41. But know this threefold course of transmigrations that depends on the (three) qualities (to be again) threefold, low, middling, and high, according to the particular nature of the acts and of the knowledge (of each man).

42. Immovable (beings), insects, both small and great, fishes, snakes, and tortoises, cattle and wild animals, are the lowest conditions to which (the quality of) Darkness leads.

43. Elephants, horses, Śūdras, and despicable barbarians, lions, tigers, and boars (are) the middling states, caused by (the quality of) Darkness.

44. Kāraṇas, Suparṇas and hypocrites, Rākṣasas and Piśācas (belong to) the highest (rank of) conditions among those produced by Darkness.

45. Jhallas, Mallas, Naṭas, men who subsist by despicable occupations and those addicted to gambling and drinking (form) the lowest (order of) conditions caused by Activity.

46. Kings and Kṣatriyas, the domestic priests of kings, and those who delight in the warfare of disputations (constitute) the middling (rank of the) states caused by Activity.

47. The Gandharvas, the Guhyakas, the servants of the gods, likewise the Apsarases, (belong all to) the highest (rank of) conditions produced by Activity.

48. Hermits, ascetics, Brāhmaṇas, the crowds of the Vaimānika deities, the lunar mansions, and the Daityas (form) the first (and lowest rank of the) existences caused by Goodness.

49. Sacrifices, the sages, the gods, the Vedas, the heavenly lights, the years, the manes, and the Sādhyas (constitute) the second order of existences, caused by Goodness.

50. The sages declare Brahmā, the creator of the universe, the law, the Great One, and the Undiscernible One (to constitute) the highest order of beings produced by Goodness.

51. Thus (the result) if the threefold action, the whole system of transmigrations which (consists) of three classes, (each) with three subdivisions, and which includes all created beings, has been fully pointed out.

— *Manusmṛti* XII.1-51; tr. G. Bühler[12]

---

12. G. Bühler, tr., *The Laws of Manu*, Delhi: Motilal Banarsidass, 1964, first published 1886, pp. 483-95, diacritics added.

11

Karma

I

THE origin of the doctrine of *karma* is uncertain. Its first unambiguous iteration is found in the *Bṛhadāraṇyaka Upaniṣad* under suggestive circumstances. The sage Yājñavalkya is being questioned, at the court of King Janaka, by another sage Ārtabhāga by name. The text runs as follows:

> 1. "Yājñavalkya," said he, "when the voice of a dead man goes into fire, his breath into wind, his eye into the sun, his mind into the moon, his hearing into the quarters of heaven, his body into the earth, his soul (*ātman*) into space, the hairs of his head into plants, the hair of his body into trees, and his blood and semen are placed in water, what then becomes of his person (*puruṣa*)?"
>
> "Ārtabhāga, my dear, take my hand. We two only will know of this. This is not for us two [to speak of] in public."
>
> The two went away and deliberated. What they said was *karma* (action). What they praised was *karma*. Verily, one becomes good by good action, bad by bad action.
>
> Thereupon Jāratkārava Ārtabhāga held his peace.

— *Bṛhadāraṇyaka Upaniṣad,* III.2.13;
translated by R.E. Hume[1]

1. R.E. Hume, tr., *The Thirteen Principal Upaniṣads*, London: Oxford University Press, 1968 (1921), p. 110.

A.L. Basham comments:

> If we are to take this passage at its face value the doctrine of *karman* was invented by Yājñavalkya, for when he said, "We two alone must know about this," he was, at the time, the *only* person who knew the secret. We note that the compiler has carefully avoided giving Yājñavalkya's words. He has literary skills and thinks logically, and if he had purported to give Yājñavalkya's exact words, as he does elsewhere, it would be evident that either a third party had listened to the conversation or Jāratkārava had betrayed the secret. This passage, as a portrayal of the author or compiler of the doctrine, represents the very beginning of the doctrine of *karman*.[2]

He then goes on to say:

> Thus, if we take these passages at face value, the doctrine of transmigration was first promulgated by Yājñavalkya, who first divulged it only to one chosen disciple but later allowed it to become more or less public. The historicity of these passages, however, is at best dubious. They probably represent the teachings of Yājñavalkya, but the circumstances in which he taught them suggest the work of an editor endowed with considerable creativity.[3]

However, as early as 1937, Bimala Churn Law drew attention to the fact that although

> Buddha is generally credited with the propounding of this doctrine . . . there is a clear statement in the *Majjhima Nikāya* . . . that the doctrine was propounded before the advent of the Buddha by an Indian teacher who was a householder.[4]

---

2. A.L. Basham, *The Origins and Developments of Classical Hinduism*, p. 44.
3. Ibid., p. 45.
4. Bimala Churn Law, *Concepts of Buddhism*, Leiden: Kern Institute, 1937, p. 54.

He identifies this householder with Yājñavalkya, who, in the *Bṛhadāraṇyaka Upaniṣad,*[5] is indeed depicted as one.[6]

II

In the same Upaniṣad, the doctrine is expounded openly and in greater detail. The account begins with the approach of death. A person is about to die . . .

The point of his heart becomes lighted up. By that light the self departs, either by the eye, or by the head, or by other bodily parts. After him, as he goes out, the life (*prāṇa*) goes out. After the life, as it goes out, all the breaths (*prāṇa*) go out. He becomes one with intelligence. What has intelligence departs with him. His knowledge and his works and his former intelligence [i.e. instinct] lay hold of him.

The Soul of the Unreleased after Death

3. Now as a caterpillar, when it has come to the end of a blade of grass, in taking the next step draws itself together towards it, just so, this soul in taking the next step, strikes down this body, dispels its ignorance, and draws itself together [for making the transition].
4. As a goldsmith, taking a piece of gold, reduces it to another newer and more beautiful form, just so this soul, striking down this body and dispelling its ignorance, makes for itself another newer and more beautiful form like that either of the fathers, or of the Gandharvas, or of the gods, or of Prajāpati, or of Brahma, or of other beings.
5. Verily, this soul is Brahma, made of knowledge, of mind, of breath, of seeing, of hearing, of earth, of water, of wind, of space, of energy and of non-energy,

5. Ibid., p. 56.
6. R.E. Hume, tr., op. cit., p. 147.

of desire and of non-desire, of anger and of non-anger, of virtuousness and of non-virtuousness. It is made of everything. This is what is meant by the saying "made of this, made of that".

According as one acts, according as one conducts himself, so does he become. The doer of good becomes good. The doer of evil becomes evil. One becomes virtuous by virtuous action, bad by bad action.

But people say: "A person is made [not of acts, but] of desires only." [In reply to this I say:] As is his desire, such is his resolve; as his resolve, such the action he performs; what action (*karma*) he performs, that he procures for himself.

6. On this point there is this verse:

When one's mind is attached — the inner self
Goes thereto with action, being attached to it alone.
Obtaining the end of his action,
Whatever he does in his world,
He comes again from that world
To this world of action.
— So the man who desires.

The Soul of the Released

Now the man who does not desire. He who is without desire, who is freed from desire, whose desire is satisfied, whose desire is the Soul — his breaths do not depart.

Being the very Brahma, he goes to Brahma.

7. On this point there is this verse:

When are liberated all
The desires that lodge in one's heart,
Then a mortal becomes immortal!
Therein he reaches Brahma!

As the slough of a snake lies on an ant-hill, dead, cast off, even so lies his body. But this incorporeal, immortal Life (*prāṇa*) is Brahmā indeed, is light indeed.

"I will give you, noble sir, a thousand [cows]", said Janaka, [king] of Videha.

— *Bṛhadāraṇyaka* IV.4.2-7; translated by R.E. Hume[7]

III

Another early Upaniṣad in which the doctrine of *karma* can be identified is the *Chāndogya*. The background of the discussion, as with the *Bṛhadāraṇyaka*, is not without an interest of its own and may be summarised as follows:

Śvetaketu once visited the assembly of the Pañcāla tribe, no doubt as a qualified brāhmaṇa, hoping to obtain largesse from them. A certain chieftain named Pravāhaṇa Jaivāli noticed him. Jaivāli, a kṣatriya, put a number of blunt questions to the young brāhmaṇa, in an abrupt manner that did not indicate great respect: "Do you know how beings go away in different directions when they die? . . . Do you know how that world up there is not filled up by all the many souls that are constantly departing from here? . . . Do you know how to get to the Path of the Gods or the Path of the Fathers?" Śvetaketu had to admit that, though he had been taught by his father all the brāhmaṇic lores, he could not answer any of these questions. Jaivāli offered to teach him his secrets, but the young man was thoroughly offended at the thought of being instructed by a kṣatriya and hurried back to his father in annoyance. He told his father how the kṣatriya Jaivāli had presumed to ask him questions he could not answer. Uddālaka, the father, could not answer them either, and he suggested to his son that they should both go and sit at the feet of the warrior chief and learn his new lore. The young man would not consent to do anything so humiliating, so the father went

7. R.E. Hume, tr., op. cit., pp. 140-41.

alone to Jaivāli's court. The kṣatriya was at first disinclined to teach the brāhmaṇa, but the latter asked him so politely that he agreed, saying, "I hope you and your ancestors won't do us any harm as a result of this. This wisdom has hitherto never been known by any brāhmaṇa, but who could refuse you when you ask so politely?"[8] Thereupon Pravāhaṇa Jaivāli, after allegorising the "yonder world", the rain-cloud, the earth, man and woman as a sacrificial fire,[9] explained:

1. So those who know this, and those too who worship in a forest with the thought that "Faith is austerity", pass into the flame [of the cremation fire]; from the flame, into the day; from the day, into the half-month of the waxing moon; from the half-month of the waxing moon, into the six months during which the sun moves northward;

2. from those months, into the year; from the year, into the sun; from the sun, into the moon; from the moon, into the lightning. There is a person (*puruṣa*) who is non-human (*a-mānava*). He leads them on to Brahma. This is the way leading to the gods.

3. But those, who in the village reverence a belief in sacrifice, merit, and almsgiving — they pass into

---

8. A.L. Basham, op. cit., pp. 45-46.

9. These allegories really constitute a metaphorical explanation of birth. "The birth of a child takes place as a result of a process interpreted as a series of sacrifices. In heaven the gods offer their faith and produce Soma (here a god, not a plant). In mid-space they offer Soma in the rain clouds, which are thought of as fiery because they contain lightning. On earth they offer the rain, and thus food is produced. In man they offer food, and semen is produced. In woman they offer the man's semen, and a child is produced. He lives his life and dies. Then his body 'is carried off to the pyre, to go to the allotted place whence he came'." (A.L. Basham, op. cit., p. 46).

smoke; from the smoke, into the night; from the night, into the latter half of the month; from the latter half of the month, into the six months during which the sun moves southward — these do not reach the year;

4. from those months, into the world of the fathers; from the world of the fathers, into the space; from the space, into the moon. That is King Soma. That is the food of the gods. The gods eat that.

5. After having remained in it as long as there is a residue [of their good works], then by that course by which they came, they return again, just as they came, into space; from space, into wind. After having become wind, one becomes smoke. After having become smoke, he becomes mist.

6. After having become mist, he becomes cloud. After having become cloud, he rains down. They are born here as rice and barley, as herbs and trees, as sesame plants and beans. Thence, verily, indeed, it is difficult to emerge; for only if someone or other eats him as food and emits him as semen, does he develop further.

7. Accordingly, those who are of pleasant conduct here — the prospect is, indeed, that they will enter a pleasant womb, either the womb of a Brāhmaṇa, or the womb of a Kṣatriya, or the womb of a Vaiśya. But those who are of a stinking conduct here — the prospect is, indeed, that they will enter a stinking womb, either the womb of a dog, or the womb of a swine, or the womb of an outcast (*caṇḍāla*).

8. But on neither of these ways are the small, continually returning creatures, [those of whom it is said:] "Be born, and die" — theirs is a third state.

   Thereby [it comes about that] yonder world is not filled up.

Therefore one should seek to guard himself. As to this there is the following verse:

9. The plunderer of gold, the liquor-drinker,

The invader of a teacher's bed, the Brahman-killer —

These four sink downward in the scale,
And, fifth, he who consorts with them.

10. But he who knows these five fires thus, is not stained with evil, even though consorting with those people. He becomes pure, clean, possessor of a pure world, who knows this — yea, he who knows this!

— *Chāndogya Upaniṣad* V.10.1-10; tr. R.E. Hume[10]

The passage is very significant both in the eschatology and philosophy of Hinduism. The distinction between the "path of the gods" and the "path of the manes" remained a major feature of Hindu eschatology, although it was ultimately overtaken by the doctrine of *karma*, which was then used to provide a philosophical basis for the doctrine of *varṇa*: a person's birth in a particular *varṇa* was attributed to the quality of the person's *karma* in the past life or lives.

IV

It should not be overlooked that in the Upaniṣads, the operation of the doctrine of *karma* is associated not merely with deeds but also with knowledge, although the word *karma* by itself means action or deeds. It subsequently came to include actions of all kinds — physical, verbal, or mental as will become apparent from a reading which follows. It should be noted that, by introducing knowledge or thoughts as a variable, an excessively mechanical interpretation of the doctrine is averted, as the "character which is determinative of one's position in the next life is formed not only by action but also

10. R.E. Hume, tr., op. cit., pp. 232-34, diacritics added, some works italicized.

by knowledge".[11] The following passages are quite explicit in this respect:

> Look (here). I shall explain to you the mystery of *Brahman*, the eternal, and also how the soul fares, after reaching death, O Gautama.
>
> Some souls enter into a womb for embodiment; others enter stationary objects according to their deeds and according to their thoughts.
>
> — *Kaṭha Upaniṣad* II.2.6-7; tr. S. Radhakrishnan[12]
>
> Either as a worm, or as an insect or as a fish or as a bird, or as a lion, or as a boar, or as a snake, or as a tiger, or as a person or as some other in this or that combination he is born again according to his deeds, according to his knowledge. . . .
>
> — *Kauṣītaki-Brāhmaṇa Upaniṣad* I.2; tr. S. Radhakrishnan[13]

V

The doctrine of *karma* undergoes elaboration both in terms of deeds or action and thoughts or knowledge. The passages from the *Manusmṛti* cited in the previous chapter (section V) represent its elaboration along these lines.[14]

VI

The idea of knowledge, inasmuch as knowledge also came to be associated with knowledge of *Brahman*, acquired a twofold meaning in the Upaniṣads — the higher (*parā*) and the lower (*aparā*). Lower knowledge did keep one confined to *saṁsāra* but higher knowledge led to liberation. The locus classicus of this distinction is *Muṇḍaka Upaniṣad* I.3-5:

---

11. R.E. Hume, tr., op. cit., p. 56.
12. S. Radhakrishnan, ed., *The Principal Upaniṣads*, p. 638.
13. Ibid., p. 754.
14. Louis Renou, ed., *Hinduism*, p. 117.

3. Śaunaka, verily, indeed, a great householder, approached Aṅgiras according to rule, and asked: "Through understanding of what, pray, does all this world become understood, sir?"

Two Kinds of Knowledge: The Traditions of Religion, and the Knowledge of the Eternal

4. To him then he said: "There are two knowledges to be known — as indeed the knowers of Brahma are wont to say: a higher (*parā*) and also a lower (*aparā*).

5. Of these, the lower is the Rig-Veda, the Yajur-Veda, the Sāma-Veda and the Atharva-Veda,

   Pronunciation (*śikṣā*), Ritual (*kalpa*), Grammar (*vyākaraṇa*),

   Definition (*nirukta*), Metrics (*chandas*), and Astrology (*jyotiṣa*)

   Now, the higher is that whereby that imperishable (*akṣara*) is apprehended". — Tr. R.E. Hume[15]

This knowledge of the imperishable confers immortality, but it can also be bewildering as Yājñavalkya's wife discovered, in a passage also cited earlier.

12. It is — as the uniting-place of all waters is the sea,
    likewise the uniting-place of all touches is the skin;
    likewise the uniting-place of all tastes is the tongue;
    likewise the uniting-place of all odours is the nose;
    likewise the uniting-place of all forms is the eye;
    likewise the uniting-place of all sounds is the ear;
    likewise the uniting-place of all intentions is the mind;
    likewise the uniting-place of all knowledges is the heart;
    likewise the uniting-place of all actions is the hands;

15. R.E. Hume, tr., op. cit., pp. 366-67.

likewise the uniting-place of all pleasures is the generative organ;
likewise the uniting-place of all evacuations is the anus;
likewise the uniting-place of all journeys is the feet;
likewise the uniting-place of all Vedas is speech.

13. It is — as is a mass of salt, without inside, without outside, entirely a mass of taste, even so, verily, is the Soul, without inside, without outside, entirely a mass of knowledge.

Arising out of these elements, into them also one vanishes away. After death there is no consciousness (*saṁjñā*). Thus, lo, said I." Thus spoke Yājñavalkya.

14. Then said Maitreyī: "Herein, indeed, you have caused me, sir, to arrive at the extreme of bewilderment. Verily, I understand It [i.e. this *Ātman*] not."

Then said he: "Lo, verily, I speak not bewilderment. Imperishable, lo, verily, is this Soul, and of indestructible quality."

— *Bṛhadāraṇyaka Upaniṣad* IV.12-14; tr. R.E. Hume[16]

VII

The appropriation of the doctrine of *karma* at the more popular level may be illustrated with the help of the following story as narrated by a Swami (who has since passed away) and faithfully taped by an anthropologist, in which the doctrine figures more playfully and less solemnly without, however, lessening its appeal.

There was a Seth [wealthy proprietor; merchant]. The Seth's name was Nagpal.

[We laugh, for Nagpal is a wealthy industrialist known to

16. R.E. Hume, tr., op. cit., pp. 146-47. This passage has been cited earlier, as part of the larger context in which it appears, in Chapter 2.

most visitors. "Not your Bombay Nagpal," Swamiji assured. "Yes?"]

He lived in Ujjain. He was a very wealthy Seth. He built many houses.

["Did you hear this story?" Swamiji looks around through his glasses. Heads shake: No, Swamiji resumes, the smile broadening on his face.]

He built a house, a house that was very beautiful. He called in many skilled craftsmen. There was no other house like this in Ujjain. After building this house, there was still a little work left before it was completed. Just one or two days of work was left. Statues had been made all over the house: statues. Many statues had been made. They all had to be painted. Then he was telling the craftsmen, "Look brothers, this house, my house, has turned out beautifully. No one here in Ujjain has a house like this. Even the government doesn't have buildings like this."

Those people said [respectfully], "This is true, Maharaj."

"As you paint these, give them the kind of colour that will last for seven generations. It should appear very beautiful. For seven generations!"

[Kirin has been waiting for Swamiji to finish the last few lines before she translates, but he turns to her clarifying the Hindi *pīṛhī* with the English word "relation." "Generation!" amends Kirin. Swamiji nods, his attention flickering from her back into the plot.]

"It should stay that beautiful." Just as he was finishing saying this, a Babaji like our Sadananda arrived there.

[Sadananda's eyebrows lift and he grins. He is a long-limbed, bearded man on the verge of middle age, with an ochre cloth wrapped around his waist.]

He arrived there and saw them just as the king was finishing what he said. Not the king, the Seth. [Swamiji hastily corrects, "The Seth, the Seth."] The Sadhu witnessed this. He laughed. He laughed inside his mind. Then he walked away.

The Seth saw him. "Why did this Maharaj laugh? What does this Babaji know? Babajis only know how to eat off other people! [We laugh.] What does he know about this house? He just laughed for no reason. He doesn't even know how to wear proper clothes!" ["Bhavani" lets out a chortle, possibly because Swamiji himself can be somewhat "topsy-turvy" in his appearance.] He kept quiet. But it stuck in his mind, "What did I do wrong? Why did he laugh?"

Then, he had a shop, a big shop. In the morning, he would give work to everyone then go and sit in the shop. He went there and sat down [Swamiji sneezes, then resumes], and as he sat . . . his business went on, tens of thousands of rupees of business. In front of him, all his employees packed things up; they filled trucks of goods: all this went on. The Seth was sitting inside. There was a space for the Seth to sit and he was sitting there. He was keeping track of the cash.

Just then a goat, you know, came running up to the Seth. He came and stood this close to him — [Swamiji's hands move to his right shoulder]. Behind him was a man who slaughters goats: a butcher! ["Slaughter" echoes Gupta Seth, addressing himself to Kirin.] He came in, too. He said, "Seth, this is my goat, and I was taking him to be slaughtered. He slipped out of my hands and came up to you. Just push him out please. I want to take him to be slaughtered."

It came into the Seth's mind, "This goat has come to me. It's my job to save his life. Then, too, I am so rich." He asked the butcher, "How much does this goat cost? Let him go and I'll give you the money."

He said, "Maharaj, give me fifteen gold coins [*mohur*] for him."

[Kirin blithely mistranslates gold coin (*mohur*) as peacock (*mor*). "*Mohur, mohur*", corrects Meena Gupta grinning from beside Kirin. "Not peacock!" says Gupta Saheb in English. "What's a *mohur*, Swamiji?" Kirin asks in confusion. "Gold coin", Gupta Saheb explains. "Not just gold", Swamiji explains. "When you say one *mohur* you mean about four rupees. So fifteen *mohur* means sixty rupees, Yes?"]

"Give me that much money, and I'll leave the goat for you", he said.

It's a habit of Seths to think, "Why fifteen gold coins for a goat?" [Amusement ripples from the Indians listening, for merchants are proverbially stingy.] He said, "I'll give you fourteen gold coins for him". If you say ten rupees, it's their habit to say five!

["They want to negotiate", Gupta Saheb clarifies in English.]

The Seth said fourteen. The butcher said, "Maharaj you won't get him for fourteen. There's fifteen rupees worth of mutton in this goat: fifteen gold coins. I brought him just after weighing him. If I slaughter him and sell the flesh, it's worth sixty rupees. That is rightfully mine. Now, if you give me that much, I'll give him to you. Otherwise, I can't give him to you." He said this once.

"Fourteen", said the Seth. Then he thought, "Whose goat is this anyway, and why pay money for him?" He didn't want to give even fourteen rupees. [We know Swamiji, means *mohur*, but no one corrects him. We laugh again, for the Seth is acting up to the tight-fisted stereotype.] "I don't want to slaughter this or anything else: what do I have to do with this goat? Why waste money for no reason?" So he thought, "Somehow I should take back my words." He said, "If you want to give him to me for fourteen *mohurs* then hand him over, otherwise take your goat away."

He said, "I won't give him up for fourteen *mohurs*. If you won't pay fifteen, give back the goat."

He said, "Fine. Take your goat away." He grabbed the goat by the ears and handed him over like this [Swamiji extends both hands.]

As he was handing him over, just then the Babaji came up in front of him. The Babaji saw him doing this. The Babaji looked at him and laughed. As he was handing him over [Swamiji's hands are frozen in front of him and his head turns towards Sadananda], he saw the Babaji. The Babaji was laughing. He thought, "I've seen the Babaji again, what's going on? The Babaji is laughing". Then he remained silent. The Babaji went away.

Then, after doing all his business, the Seth went home around twelve or one o'clock. That day it was one year since his child was born. He had just one son. For a long time, he had no children.

His wife was waiting for her husband to return. She had cooked nice food. It was a year since the child's birth, ["Burtha-day" Swamiji explains in English. Bhavani lets out a low, delighted chuckle]. As the husband was coming, she had set out a silver plate [*thālī*]. When he saw his father, the baby wiggled his head like this — [Swamiji bobs in his seat, shaking his shoulders, rolling his head] — the baby who was sitting in his mother's lap. She had made all kinds of preparations, was doing all kinds of things, had set out lots of fine sweets. She served sweets, she served fried bread [*pūrī*], she served all kinds of good things for her husband to eat. He was eating.

The baby was sitting in his mother's lap, wiggling his head, jumping around. [Swamiji demonstrates: an oversized infant wearing ochre. Watching him, it is impossible not to laugh.] He was jumping, the way babies do, pushing up straight [hunching his back, then suddenly flexing it; arms raised from the elbows and clenched at the fists.] When his mother saw this, she said, "Look how happy this child is when he sees you!"

He said [reaching out his hands], "Give him to me". He sat the baby down on his lap.

"Now you too feed him a bite or two since he's one year old", she said. So he also put a bit of those sweets into the baby's mouth. [Left elbow crooked as though supporting the baby, Swamiji thrusts the bunched fingers of his right hand toward it.] It was a baby. You have love for a baby, don't you? Just then — it's baby habit — he let out a stream of pee — *chullllll!* [Swamiji flings out his hand to show how far the pee went. Along with him, we are helplessly laughing.] When he peed, it fell all over his father's clothes.

"*Che-che* he's peed!" he did this [distastefully flicking and wiping at his robes, then swiftly depositing the imaginary bundle over the edge of the chair.] When babies pee, you know, they pee quite a distance! Some fell on the plate, too. "What has this baby done peeing?" he said.

His wife said, "So what if he peed, he's your own child". She took the baby back.

Then he was sitting there eating from that very plate. The food that had been peed upon was on one side, and he was eating from that very side. Not too much pee, just a little had fallen on the food.

Just then, once again the Babaji appeared. "Give me alms", [*bhavati bhikṣām dehi*] he called. Yes? The Seth heard this as he was eating. It was the same Babaji. The Babaji was laughing from over there.

Then he couldn't endure this any more in his mind. "I've seen him *three times* today, and all the three times this Babaji has laughed! I must have made some kind of mistake, and that's why this Babaji is laughing. There seems to be some secret on his lips." So he immediately left his food. He went and prostrated at the Babaji's feet. "Babaji, what's going on? I've had *darśana* of your's three times. I'm very fortunate to have done so. All three times you laughed; there seems to be some secret hidden on your lips. You're not saying anything. Why do you laugh? What is the reason? Tell me, what wrong did I do?"

He said, "It's nothing, *jī*. We *sādhu*s are always laughing".

"No, no. There's something or the other in your laughter. You'll have to tell me."

He said, "If you want me to tell you why, you must come alone in the evening to the banks of the Sipra river. ['The Sipra river in Ujjain', Swamiji adds as an aside.] Come, and I'll tell you: at five o'clock."

"Fine", the Seth said.

He went there at exactly five o'clock. Talking away, the two of them walked some distance along the river bank. When they reached a deserted place, the Seth caught hold of the Babaji's feet. "Now tell me, why did you laugh?"

The Babaji said, "Forget about it, *jī*, why do you ask about everything? I just laughed for no particular reason."

"No, no, you must tell me something."

"What's this about? What should I tell you? Ask me."

He said, "This morning, as I was telling the employees to paint the statues. At that time, you looked at me, laughed, and went away. You didn't say anything, you just looked, laughed, and left. What was the reason for this?"

["I'll give you a banana, doctor Sahib", Swamiji motions to the doctor's youngest son who had come in with his lunch and is now slipping out the door. "I'll give you a nice banana." He breaks one from the bunch and hands it over as he continues speaking.]

The Babaji said, "Look, it's like this. What I specially saw was the great hopes a soul [*jīva*] has. You're going to die in seven days. You're thinking about seven generations. After you die, how does what becomes of the house matter to you? Why are you worrying about seven generations now? When I saw this, it made me laugh. You'll die in seven days and you are thinking about seven generations!"

"Will I die in seven days?!" [eyes widened with alarm.]

"O yes!" [Swamiji's droll enunciation of English makes us all — especially the Westerners — laugh.]

"All right *jī*, let's forget that." [Swamiji's voice drops into a mumbling, worried undertone, hand to his chin. We sit silent. There is a pause, and then his voice gathers strength for the next question.] "Then, when I was sitting in the shop and handing over the goat; at that time you laughed. Why was this?"

"Forget that, *jī*, forget it", he said.

The Seth said, "You have to tell me that, too".

"Do you know who that goat is?" he asked.

"Who is he?"

"He's your father", the Babaji said.

"My father!" [Swamiji stares with alarm. Another wave of laughter breaks into the room.]

He said, "That butcher was a porter before. Your father told a lie about Rs. 60, he wrote this off and embezzled it from him; he wrote false accounts. Your father did a bad thing with this money when he embezzled it. Then your father died. When he died, according to his past actions [*karma*] he took birth as a goat. Then, the man who had been a porter couldn't earn enough and started working as a butcher instead. Now your father was a goat. He had to repay the money; the goat was caught. He had to repay the money, right? What does a goat have? His mutton would have to be sold. "I gave my children great riches. My child will release me": he thought so and came to you!

[Here Kirin's tape snapped to the end, and, turning it over, she missed recording the next line: "The butcher asked for fifteen gold coins but you only want to give fourteen"].

"If you had only given the fifteenth gold coin your father would have been saved. You were miserly about four rupees, though you had eaten so much of his wealth — just because of four rupees you couldn't save your father. He had to give his mutton to free himself of the debt. [Swamiji laughs now, amusement bubbling between his words.] By dying, he could return the debt. It was paid off."

And the third thing the Seth asked was, "When I was at home, why did you laugh? The time I was eating my food."

He said, "Just forget about that, *jī*".

"No, you must tell me that, too."

"Do you know who your child is? Do you know why your child looked at you and laughed?"

He said, "What is it?"

"That child was your wife's lover in the past. He loved her. You had money in hand, you had him murdered. To take his revenge this man took birth as your child, in your house. You killed him then, and now he sits on your wife's lap! When he sees you, he wiggles his head, he laughs. [Laughter — especially from the women.] 'Now, what will you do to me? I sit here with such authority. Watch, I'll show you. You've talked about seven generations; in one generation I'll ruin your name. I'll make your name a bad name. I'll finish off all your wealth.' The child looks at you saying this. Then as you sit and feed him — you eat off a silver plate, right? — he says, 'Eat my piss' and he pees. [Laughter shakes the room.] You feed him with love. When I saw this, it made me laugh. You couldn't save your father because of four rupees; your enemy pees and you eat it! Thinking about the ways of the world, I laughed. No one knows what lies ahead. The Lord's play is strange and marvellous [*ajab*]. This is what made me laugh."

He said [brow laden with worry], "Will I really die in seven days?"

"You'll certainly die."

"How will I die?"

"You'll have a sharp pain in your head. [Kirin hesitates while translating and Swamiji proffers in English "headache!"] You'll die because of this."

"If this is so, then what should I do?"

"Since this is so, you should divide your riches into four portions. One portion should be given to the poor. One portion should be kept for your wife and child. One portion should be given to a temple or a mosque. And one portion should be given to some friend or old person. Then this will all be of use to you. You'll definitely die."

That story is now finished.[17]

17. Kirin Narayan, *Storytellers, Saints, and Scoundrels: Folk Narrative in Hindu Religious Teaching*, Delhi: Motilal Banarsidass, 1992, pp. 161-67.

12

Dharma

The concept of *dharma* is one of the most comprehensive and pervasive concepts of Hinduism, and ranges from Hinduism itself being a *dharma*, a particular instantiation of *dharma* understood as a religion in the Western sense — a comparatively recent understanding — to various kinds of *dharma*. The word is derived from a root which means to uphold so that whatever upholds the cosmos, society, polity, individuality, morality, *zeitgeist*, etc. qualifies as *dharma*, indeed even what holds one up in a crisis; and the term can function both descriptively and normatively according to the context, although the usage in general tends to be normative.

I

The cosmic dimension of *dharma* is already apparent in the Vedic times, as in the following stanza addressed to Varuṇa.

> Rich in *ghee* [i.e., clarified butter considered as fertilising rain], exceedingly glorious among beings, wide, broad, honey-dispensing, with beautiful forms, Heaven and Earth are, in accordance with Varuṇa's cosmic law (*dharma*), held asunder, both ageless and rich in seed.
>
> — R̥g-Veda VI.70; tr. R.N. Dandekar[1]

II

The form in which society is upheld by *dharma* is known as *varṇāśrama dharma* or the duties of "caste" and stages of life.

1. Wm Theodore de Bary et al., eds., *Sources of Indian Tradition* (2nd edn.), New York: Columbia University Press, 1958, p. 10.

The *āśrama dharma*s are covered in detail in a later chapter; one may focus here on the *varṇa dharma*s, which consist of a description of duties of the four *varṇa*s namely brāhmaṇa, kṣatriya, vaiśya and śūdra. One notes that, depending on the text and its concerns, they tend to be described in terms of general moral duties or specific occupational concerns, with the following famous passages from the *Bhagavad-Gītā* blending the two (XVIII:41-44).

41. The actions of the brāhmaṇa, the warrior [kṣatriya], the artisan [vaiśya] and the serf [śūdra] are apportioned, O Paraṁtapa, according to the primary constituents arising [in their] own being (*svabhāva*).

42. Calm, restraint, austerity, purity, patience and uprightness, knowledge (*vijñāna*), belief-in-God (*āstikya*) — these are brāhmaṇa-actions, born of the own-being of a brāhmaṇa.

43. Courage, vigour, steadfastness, resourcefulness, unwillingness — to flee even in battle,

    Generosity and lordly disposition (*Īśvara bhāva*) [these are] the actions [characteristics] of a warrior [kṣatriya], born of [his] own-being.

44. Agriculture (*kṛṣi*), tending cattle, trade, [these are] the actions of a merchant [vaiśya], born of his own-being. Action of the nature of service is born of the own-being of a serf (śūdra).[2]

The following description of the duties of the vaiśya and śūdra from the *Manusmṛti*, a text specifically devoted to social ordering, is predictably more detailed:

---

2. Georg Feuerstein, *The Bhagavad-Gītā: Yoga of Contemplation and Action*, New Delhi: Arnold-Heinemann [India] Pvt. Ltd., 1980, p. 155, with slight modification.

IX. 325. Thus the eternal law concerning the duties of a king has been fully declared; known that the following rules apply in (due) order to the duties of vaiśyas and śūdras.

326. After a vaiśya has received the sacraments and has taken a wife, he shall be always attentive to the business, whereby he may subsist and to (that of) tending cattle.

327. For when the Lord of creatures (Prajāpati) created cattle, he made them over to the vaiśya; to the brāhmaṇa, and to the king he entrusted all created beings.

328. A vaiśya must never (conceive this) wish, "I will not keep cattle"; and if a vaiśya is willing (to keep them), they must never be kept by (men of) other (castes).

329. (A vaiśya) must know the respective value of gems, of pearls, of coral, of metals, of (cloth) made of thread, of perfumes, and of condiments.

330. He must be acquainted with (the manner of) sowing of seeds, and of the good and bad qualities of fields, and he must perfectly know all measures and weights.

331. Moreover, the excellence and defects of commodities, the advantages and disadvantages of (different) countries, the (probable) profit and loss of merchandise, and the means of properly rearing cattle.

332. He must be acquainted with the (proper) wages of servants, with the various languages of men, with the manner of keeping goods, and (the rules of) purchase and sale.

333. Let him exert himself to the utmost in order to increase his property in a righteous manner, and let him zealously give food to all created beings.

334. But to serve brāhmaṇas (who are) learned in the

Vedas, householders, and famous (for virtue) is the highest duty of a śūdra, which leads to beatitude.

335. (A śūdra who is) pure, the servant of his betters, gentle in his speech, and free from pride, and always seeks a refuge with brāhmaṇas, attains (in his next life) a higher caste.

336. The excellent law for the conduct of the (four) castes (varṇa), (when they are) not in distress, has been thus promulgated . . .

— *Manusmṛti* XI.325-336; tr. G. Bühler[3]

III

The manner in which *dharma* upholds polity is through the *rājadharma,* or the duties of kings in particular, and the duties of the ruling class or *kṣatriyadharma* in general. But it also upholds polity in a subtler way — as the principle underlying justice, according to the following Upaniṣadic account. The word *dharma* has been translated as justice in the concluding section.

11. Verily, in the beginning this (world) was *Brahman*, one only. That, being one, did not flourish. He created further an excellent form, the *Kṣatra* power, even those who are *Kṣatra*s (rulers) among the gods, Indra, Varuṇa, Soma (Moon), Rudra, Parjanya, Yama, Mṛtyu (Death), Īśāna. Therefore, there is nothing higher than *Kṣatra*. Therefore, at the Rājasūya sacrifice the brāhmaṇa sits below the kṣatriya. On kṣātrahood alone does he confer this honour. But the brāhmaṇa is nevertheless the source of the *Kṣatra*. Therefore, even if the king attains supremacy at the end of it, he resorts to the Brāhmaṇa as his source. Therefore he who injures the Brāhmaṇa strikes at his own source. He becomes more evil as he injures one who is superior.

---

3. G. Bühler, tr., *The Laws of Manu*, pp. 400-01, diacritics added.

12. Yet he did not flourish. He created the *viś* (the commonality), these classes of gods who are designated in groups. The Vasus, Rudras, Ādityas, Viśvedevas and Maruts.

13. He did not still flourish. He created the Śūdra order, as Pūṣan. Verily, this (earth) is Pūṣan (the nourisher), for she nourishes everything that is.

14. Yet he did not flourish. He created further an excellent form, justice. This is the power of the Kṣatriya class, viz. justice. Therefore, there is nothing higher than justice. So a weak man hopes (to defeat) a strong man by means of justice as one does through a king. Verily, that which is justice is truth. Therefore they say of a man who speaks the truth, he speaks justice or of a man who speaks justice that he speaks the truth. Verily, both these are the same.

— *Bṛhadāraṇyaka Upaniṣad* I.4.11-14;
tr. S. Radhakrishnan[4]

It is worth noting that this account of the creation of *varṇa*s differs from the earlier account of the Ṛg-Veda (X.90), in which the four classes are created simultaneously, and from a later account of the *Mahābhārata,* in which the other three castes are formed out of the brāhmaṇas — the original *varṇa* — through occupational differentiation[5]

IV

The interpretation of that crucial Sanskrit term, *svadharma,* is problematical. On the one hand, it has been argued that

> the concept of *svadharma* is a very crucial one. *Dharma* is right conduct not in a general sense but specified for each caste and for each situation in life. Time and again, the rule laid down in the *Bhagavad-Gītā* is quoted: 'It is better to fulfil

4. S. Radhakrishnan, ed., *The Principal Upaniṣads*, pp. 169-70.
5. Louis Renou, ed., *Hinduism*, pp. 141-43.

one's own duties (*dharma*), however imperfectly, than to do that of another, however perfect it may be.'[6]

This common position poses some problems. For one, if *svadharma* as literally one's own *dharma*, is identical with one's *varṇa dharma*, then what is the point in distinguishing between one's own *dharma* and one's *varṇa dharma*, despite the coincidence? Is the underlying idea the following: that in times of crisis, one can take on the duties of other *varṇas*, although one still retains one's own original *varṇa*? Does this mean that one's own *dharma*, in a sense, can change? In that case the quotation from the *Bhagavad-Gītā* is difficult to apply. Moreover, that very idea is expressed in the *Dhammapada* [166], a Buddhist text which does not accept the view of Hindu Dharmaśāstras (or treatises on *dharma*) regarding *varṇa*, as follows:

> Let no one forget his own duty for the sake of another's, however great; let a man, after he has discerned his own duty, be always attentive to his duty.[7]

Thus, while *svadharma* and *varṇa dharma* may coincide, it is problematical to regard them as identical.

V

Dharma as morality has a significance all its own.

> The heart of *dharma* consisted of universal moral ideas such as truth and non-violence, self-control and charity. . . . The Dharmaśāstras call it *sādhāraṇa dharma* and the Buddhists and Jainas call it with greater accuracy, simply as *dharma*.[8]

---

6. Klaus K. Klostermaier, *A Survey of Hinduism,* Albany: State University of New York Press, 1988, p. 48. *Bhagavad-Gītā* III.35 is cited in support; XVIII.47 could also have been cited.
7. F. Max Müller, tr., *The Dhammapada*, Oxford University Press, 1881; rpt. Motilal Banarsidass, 1973, p. 46.
8. G.C. Pande, *Dimensions of Ancient Indian Social History*, New Delhi: Books & Books, 1984, p. 167.

The *Manusmṛti* shares in this accuracy, for in the ensuing extract it is the word *dharma* which has been translated as spiritual merit.

> Giving no pain to any creature, let him slowly accumulate spiritual merit, for the sake of acquiring a companion to the next world, just as the white ant gradually raises its hill.
>
> For in the next world neither father, nor mother, nor wife, nor sons, nor relations stay to be his companions; spiritual merit alone remains with him.
>
> Single is each being born; single it dies; single it enjoys the reward of its virtue; single it suffers the punishment of its sin.
>
> Leaving the dead body on the ground like a log of wood, or a clod of earth, the relatives depart with averted faces; but spiritual merit follows the soul.
>
> Let him, therefore, always slowly accumulate spiritual merit, in order that it may be his companion after death; for without merit as his companion, he will traverse a gloom difficult to traverse.
>
> That companion speedily conducts the man who is devoted to duty and effaces his sins by austerities, to the next world, radiant and clothed with an ethereal body.
>
> — *Manusmṛti* IV.238-243: tr. G. Bühler as adapted by Louis Renou[9]

VI

The idea of *yugadharma*, or the spirit of the age, represents another dimension of *dharma* in classical Hinduism. Its more formal expression is found in the idea that each of the four *yugas*, which compromise a *mahāyuga*, possess their own characteristics.

---

9. Louis Renou, ed., op. cit., pp. 122-23.

85. One set of duties (is prescribed) for men in the Kṛta age, different ones in the Tretā and in the Dvāpara, and (again) another (set) in the Kali, in proportion as (those) ages decrease in length.

86. In the Kṛta age the chief (virtue) is declared to be (the performance of) austerities, in the Tretā (divine) knowledge, in the Dvāpara (the performance of) sacrifices, in the Kali liberality alone.

— *Manusmṛti* I.85-86; tr. G. Bühler[10]

VII

Dharma is transformed in the crucible of crisis. For instance, in a crisis all the four *varṇa*s can wield arms or use force, the prerogative of the kṣatriya in normal times.

348. Twice-born men may take up arms when (they are) hindered (in the fulfilment of) their duties, when destruction (threatens) the twice-born castes (varṇa) in (evil) times.

349. In their own defence, in a strife for the fees of officiating priests, and in order to protect women and Brāhmaṇas; he who (under such circumstances) kills in the cause of right, commits no sin.

350. One may slay without hesitation an assassin who approaches (with murderous intent), whether (he be one's) teacher, a child or an aged man, or a Brāhmaṇa deeply versed in the Vedas.

351. By killing an assassin the slayer incurs no guilt, whether (he does it) publicly or secretly; in that case fury recoils upon fury.

— *Manusmṛti* VIII.348-351; tr. G. Bühler[11]

10. G. Bühler, tr., op. cit., pp. 23-24.

11. Ibid., pp. 342-43.

13

Māyā

I

Knowledge involves the overcoming of ignorance. Such ignorance of a radically metaphysical character is called *avidyā* or *māyā*. It is that which prevents one from realising *Brahman* as it is, whether *nirguṇa* or *saguṇa*. The word *māyā* becomes more prominent in subsequent literature within Hinduism than it is in the Upaniṣads, the *Brahma-Sūtra* or the *Bhagavad-Gītā*. It is, however, not entirely absent in earlier literature. For instance, in the Upaniṣads, it is clearly mentioned in both an absolutistic and theistic context, where its exact connotation may be difficult to pin down, but its general meaning is fairly clear.

It appears in the background of the following story in the *Bṛhadāraṇyaka Upaniṣad*:

> The two Aśvins desired instruction from Dadhyañc. But the latter was loath to impart it, for Indra had threatened Dadhyañc that if he ever told his honey-doctrine to anyone else, he (Indra) would cut his head off. To avoid this untoward result, the Aśvins took off Dadhyañc's head and substituted it with a horse's head. Then, after Dadhyañc had declared the honey-doctrine in compliance with their request and Indra had carried out his threat, the Aśvins restored to Dadhyañc his own head. The episode shows the extreme difficulty with which even gods secured the knowledge originally possessed by Indra.[1]

1. R.E. Hume, tr., *The Thirteen Principal Upanishads*, London, Oxford Univerisity Press, 1968 [1921], p. 104, n. 1.

The statements made by Dadhyañc to the Aśvins includes the following, which begins with a citation from the *Ṛg-Veda* (VI.47.18):

> "He became corresponding in form to every form.
> This is to be looked upon as a form of him.
> Indra by his magic powers (*māyā*) goes about in many forms;
> Yoked are his ten-hundred steeds."

> He [i.e. the Soul, *Ātman*], verily, is the steeds. He, verily, is tens and thousands, many and the endless. This Brahma is without an earlier and without a later, without an inside and without an outside. This Soul is Brahma, the all-perceiving. —Such is the instruction.
>
> — *Bṛhadāraṇyaka Upaniṣad* II.5.19; tr. R.E. Hume[2]

The concept of *māyā* is apparently an attempt to answer the question: If the ultimate reality is unitary (and not merely a unity), then how is the multiplicity of the phenomenal world to be accounted for? It is accounted for in the terms of *māyā*.

The use of *māyā*, in the theistic context, is even more explicit in the *Śvetāśvatara Upaniṣad* IV.9-10:

9. Sacred poetry (*chandas*), the sacrifices, the ceremonies, the ordinances,

   The past, the future, and what the Vedas declare —

   This whole world the illusion-maker (*māyin*) projects out of this [Brahma].

   And in it by illusion (*māyā*) the other is confined.

10. Now, one should know that Nature (*prakṛti*) is an illusion (*māyā*),

    And that the Mighty Lord (Maheśvara) is the illusion-maker (*māyin*).

    This whole world is pervaded

2. R.E. Hume, tr., *The Thirteen Principal Upanishads*, p. 105.

With beings that are parts of Him.

— Translated by R.E. Hume[3]

The following comment may be helpful here:

> God is represented as the creator of the universe, and *māyā* as the power (*śakti*) that helps him in creating it. In this form, he becomes the material as well as the efficient cause of the universe and is sometimes spoken of as the great magician who brings forth out of himself the whole spectacle of the universe. The point of the comparison with a magician is that he is in no way deluded by that spectacle as others are, for there is in his case a never-failing realisation of its actual character; and this is the reason why, as we stated above, evil does not touch him.[4]

II

Māyā can be associated with both *nirguṇa* and *saguṇa Brahman*. In association with the former, it is looked upon as the ground of the world illusion in the following way:

> What happens is this: just as the dormant power of sleep displays itself as dream, so also the dormant power of *māyā* display itself as this plurality, consisting of *Īśvara*, His will, the universe and the *jīva*s. *Īśvara* is thus the product of *māyā* and He cannot be the origin of His origin. *Māyā* therefore has no antecedent cause. In dissolution there remains only Pure Being devoid of will, and admitting of no change. In creation *māyā* hitherto remaining unmanifest in this Pure Being, shines forth as the mind. By the play of mind, plurality appears as *Īśvara*, the worlds and the *jīva*s, like magic. *Māyā* manifest is creation, and *māyā* unmanifest is dissolution. Thus of its own accord, *māyā* appears or

3. R.E. Hume, tr., *The Thirteen Principal Upanishads*, p. 404.
4. M. Hiriyanna, *The Essentials of Indian Philosophy*, p. 164.

withdraws itself and has thus no beginning. Therefore, we say there was no antecedent cause for it.

10-11. Disciple (D): What is its nature?

Master (M): It is inexpressible. Because its existence is later invalidated, it is not real; because it is factually experienced, it is not unreal; nor can it be a mixture of the two opposites the real and the unreal. Therefore, the wise say that it is indescribable (*anirvacanīya*).

D: Now what is real and what is unreal?

M: That which is the substratum of *māyā*, Pure Being or *Brahman*, admitting of no duality, is real. The illusory phenomenon, consisting of names and forms, and called the universe, is unreal.

D: What can *māyā* be said to be?

M: Neither of the two. It is different from the real substratum and also from the unreal phenomenon.

D: Please explain this.

12-17 M: Say there is fire; it is the substratum. The sparks fly off from it. They are the modifications of fire. The sparks are not seen in the fire itself, but come out of it. An observation of this phenomenon makes us infer a power inherent in fire which produces the sparks.

Clay is the substratum; a hollow sphere with a neck and open mouth is made out of it, and is called a pot. This fact makes us infer a power which is neither clay nor pot but different from the both.

Water is the substratum; bubbles are its effect; a power different from both is inferred.

A snake-egg is the substratum and a young snake is the product; a power different from the egg and the young snake is inferred.

> A seed is the substratum and the sprout, its product; a power different from the seed and the sprout is inferred.
>
> The unchanging *jīva* in deep sleep is the substratum and dream is the effect; a power different from the *jīva* and the dream is inferred after waking up from sleep.
>
> In the same way, the power lying latent in *Brahman* produces the illusion of the *jagat*. The substratum of his power is *Brahman* and the *jagat* is its effect. This power cannot be either of them, but must be different from both. It cannot be defined. However it exists. But it remains inscrutable. Therefore, we say the "nature" of *māyā* is indescribable.
>
> — *Advaita Bodha Dīpikā* II.9-17:
> tr. Sri Munagala Venkataramiah[5]

III

In association with *saguṇa Brahman* or *Īśvara*, it is often spoken of as Viṣṇu's *māyā*. Its operation in this capacity is delightfully illustrated in a parable by Ramakrishna Paramahansa (1836-1886), which is presented below as narrated by Heinrich Zimmer:

> Through prolonged austerities and devotional practices, [Nārada] had won the grace of Viṣṇu. The god had appeared before the saint in his hermitage and granted him the fulfilment of a wish. "Show me the magic power of your *māyā*", Nārada had prayed, and the god had replied, "I will. Come with me"; but again with that ambiguous smile on his beautifully curved lips.
>
> From the pleasant shadows of the sheltering hermit grove, Viṣṇu conducted Nārada across a bare stretch

5. *Advaita Bodha Dīpikā* [Lamp of Non-Dual Knowledge], Tiruvannamalai: Sri Ramanasramam, 1967, pp. 28-29. D=Disciple, M= Master.

of land which blazed like metal under the merciless glow of a scorching sun. The two were very soon very thirsty. At some distance, in the glaring light, they perceived the thatched roofs of a tiny hamlet. Viṣṇu asked: "Will you go over there and fetch me some water?"

"Certainly, O Lord," the saint replied, and he made off to the distant group of huts. The god relaxed under the shadow of a cliff, to await his return.

When Nārada reached the hamlet, he knocked at the first door. A beautiful maiden opened it to him and the holy man experienced something of which he had never up to that time dreamed: the enchantment of her eyes. They resembled those of his divine Lord and friend. He stood and gazed. He simply forgot what he had come for. The girl, gentle and candid, bade him welcome. Her voice was a golden noose about his neck. As though moving in a vision, he entered the door.

The occupants of the house were full of respect for him, yet not the least bit shy. He was honourably received, as a holy man, yet somehow not as a stranger; rather, as an old and venerable acquaintance who had been a long time away. Nārada remained with them impressed by their cheerful and noble bearing, and feeling entirely at home. Nobody asked him what he had come for; he seemed to have belonged to the family from time immemorial. And after a certain period, he asked the father for permission to marry the girl, which was no more than everyone in the house had been expecting. He became a member of the family and shared with them the age-old burdens and simple delights of a peasant household.

Twelve years passed; he had three children. When his father-in-law died, he became head of the household, inheriting the estate and managing it, tending the cattle and cultivating the fields. The twelfth year, the rainy season was extraordinarily violent: the streams swelled, torrents poured down the hills, and the little village was inundated by a sudden flood. In the night, the straw huts and the cattle were carried away and everybody fled.

With one hand supporting his wife, with the other leading two of his children, and bearing the smallest on his shoulder, Nārada set forth hastily. Forging ahead through the pitch darkness and lashed by the rain, he waded through slippery mud, staggered through whirling waters. The burden was more than he could manage with the current heavily dragging at his legs. Once, when he stumbled, the child slipped from his shoulder and disappeared in the roaring night. With a desperate cry, Nārada let go of the older children to catch hold of the smallest, but was too late. Meanwhile, the flood swiftly carried off the other two, and even before he could realise the disaster, ripped from his side his wife, swept his own feet from under him and flung him headlong in the torrent like a log. Unconscious, Nārada was stranded eventually on a little cliff. When he returned to consciousness, he opened his eyes upon a vast sheet of muddy water. He could only weep.

"Child!" He heard a familiar voice, which nearly stopped his heart. "Where is the water you went to fetch for me? I have been waiting for more than half an hour."

Nārada turned around. Instead of water he beheld the brilliant desert in the midday sun. He found the god standing at his shoulder. The cruel curves of the fascinating mouth, still smiling, parted with the gentle question: "Do you comprehend now the secret of my *māyā*?"[6]

---

6. Heinrich Zimmer, *Myths and Symbols in Indian Art and Civilization* (ed. Joseph Campbell), New York and Evanston: Harper & Row, 1962, pp. 32-34.

14

Mokṣa

I

When the *jīva* overcomes *māyā* or *avidyā*, that is, radical metaphysical ignorance about its true nature, then *saṁsāra* ceases and *mokṣa* (liberation), that is, liberation from *saṁsāra* and the sorrows it entails, is ensured. In keeping with the two modes of understanding *Brahman* — *nirguṇa* or *saguṇa* — the precise nature of liberation varies, but in both cases it involves the cessation of *saṁsāra*.

The achievement of *mokṣa* is not merely a negative one of the cessation of *saṁsāra*; it is also a positive state of bliss. This again holds true in *mokṣa* both in its absolutistic and theistic understanding.

This is the inquiry concerning bliss:

> Let there be a youth, a good youth, well read, prompt in action, steady in mind and strong in body. Let this whole earth be full of wealth for him. This is one human bliss.
>
> What is a hundred times the human bliss, that is just one bliss of human fairies — also of a man who is well versed in the Vedas and who is not smitten with desire.
>
> What is hundred times the bliss of the human fairies, that is just one bliss of the divine fairies — also of a man who is well versed in the Vedas and who is not smitten with desire. What is hundred times the bliss of the divine fairies, that is one bliss of the fathers in their long enduring world — also of a man who is well versed in the Vedas and who is not smitten with desire.

What is hundred times the bliss of the fathers in their long enduring world, that is yet again one bliss of the gods who are born so by birth, as also of a man who is well versed in the Vedas and who is not smitten with desire.

What is hundred times the bliss of the gods who are born so by birth, that is one bliss of the gods by work, who go to the gods by work, as also of a man who is well versed in the Vedas and who is not smitten with desire.

What is hundred times the bliss of the gods by work, that is again just one bliss of the gods, as also of a man who is well versed in the Vedas and who is not smitten with desire.

What is hundred times the bliss of the gods, that is one bliss of Indra — as also of a man who is well versed in the Vedas and who is not smitten with desire.

What is hundred times the bliss of Indra, that is the one bliss of Bṛhaspati — as also of a man who is well versed in the Vedas and who is not smitten with desire.

What is hundred times the bliss of Bṛhaspati, that is one bliss of Prajāpati, as also of a man who is well versed in the Vedas and who is not smitten with desire.

What is hundred times the bliss of Prajāpati, that is one bliss of Brahmā — as also of a man who is well versed in the Vedas and who is not smitten with desire.

He, who is here in the person and he who is yonder in the Sun — he is one. He, who knows this, on departing from this world, reaches to the self which consists of food, reaches the self which consists of life, reaches the self which consists of mind, reaches the self which consists of understanding, reaches the self which consists of bliss.

As to that, there is also this verse:

1. Whence words return along with the mind, not

> attaining It, he who knows that bliss of *Brahman* fears not from anything at all.
>
> — *Taittirīya Upaniṣad*, II.8.1-II.9.1; tr. S. Radhakrishnan[1]

II

The state of *mokṣa* is often described as involving *sāyujya* (union). In an absolutistic context it implies merging in the Absolute ontologically from which one was paradoxically never separated. As a theistic concept, it implies effecting a psychological union with god. The school of Kāśmīr Śaivism straddles the two; so one might begin with a description from that school by Abhinavagupta (tenth/eleventh century CE).

> When thus the imagination of quality has vanished, and he (the released soul) has surmounted the illusion of *māyā*, he is merged in *Brahman*, as water in water, milk in milk. When thus, through contemplation, the group of elements has been resolved into the substance of Śiva, what grief what delusion can befall him who surveys the universe as *Brahman*.
>
> — *Sarvadarśanasaṁgraha*: tr. E.B. Cowell and A.E. Gough[2]

III

The state of the *jīvanmukta*, or one who has realised identity with the Absolute in this very life, is described in glowing terms in the *Vivekacūḍāmaṇi*. Such a person may alternatively be characterized as possessing self-knowledge as well, for from the Absolutistic standpoint *Ātman* = *Brahman*.

---

1. S. Radhakrishnan, ed., *The Principal Upaniṣads*, Atlantic Heights, NJ, Humanities Press International, 1992 [1953], pp. 550-51.
2. Cited in T.M.P. Mahadevan, *Outlines of Hinduism*, Bombay: Chetana Ltd., 1971, p. 177.

This *Ātman* shines with its own light. Its power is infinite. It is beyond sense-knowledge. It is the source of all experience. He who knows the *Ātman* is free from every kind of bondage. He is full of glory. He is the greatest of the great.

The things perceived by the senses cause him neither grief nor pleasure. He is not attached to them. Neither does he shun them. Constantly delighting in the *Ātman* he is always at play within himself. He tastes the sweet, unending bliss of the *Ātman* and is satisfied.

The child plays with his toys, forgetting even hunger and physical pain. In like manner, the knower of *Brahman* takes his delight in the *Ātman*, forgetting all thought of "I" and "mine".

He gets his food easily by begging alms, without anxiety or care. He drinks from the clear stream. He lives unfettered and independent. He sleeps without fear in the forest or on the cremation-ground. He does not need to wash or dry his clothes, for he wears none. The earth is his bed. He walks the highway of Vedānta. His playmate is *Brahman*, the everlasting.

The knower of the *Ātman* does not identify himself with his body. He rests within it, as if within a carriage. If people provide him with comforts and luxuries, he enjoys them and plays with them like a child. He bears no outward mark of a holy man. He remains quite unattached to the things of this world.

He may wear costly clothing, or none. He may be dressed in deer or tiger skin or clothed in pure knowledge. He may seem like a madman or like a child, or sometimes like an unclean spirit. Thus, he wanders the earth.

The man of contemplation walks alone. He lives desireless amidst the objects of desire. The *Ātman* is his eternal satisfaction. He sees the *Ātman* present in all things.

Sometimes he appears to be a fool, sometimes a wise man. Sometimes he seems splendid as a king, sometimes feeble-minded. Sometimes he is calm and silent. Sometimes he draws men to him, as a python attracts its prey. Sometimes people honour him greatly, sometimes they insult him. Sometimes they ignore him. That is how the illumined soul lives, always absorbed in the highest bliss.

He has no riches, yet he is always contented. He is helpless, yet of mighty power. He enjoys nothing, yet he is continually rejoicing. He has no equal, yet he sees all men as his equals.

He acts, yet is not bound by his action. He reaps the fruit of past actions, yet is unaffected by them. He has a body, but he does not identify himself with it. He appears to be an individual, yet he is present in all things, everywhere.

The knower of *Brahman*, who lives in freedom from body-consciousness, is never touched by pleasure or pain, good or evil.

If a man identifies himself with the gross and subtle coverings within which he dwells, he will experience pleasure and pain, good or evil. But nothing is either good or evil to the contemplative sage, because he has realised the *Ātman* and his bonds have fallen from him.

During an eclipse, the shadow of the earth falls upon the sun. The ignorant, who do not understand what has happened, say that the sun has been swallowed up by the darkness of the eclipse — but the sun can never be swallowed up.

In the same manner, the ignorant see the body of a knower of *Brahman* and identify him with it. Actually, he is free from the body and every other kind of bondage. To him, the body is merely a shadow.

He dwells in the body, but regards it as a thing apart

from himself — like the cast-off skin of a snake. The body moves hither and thither, impelled by the vital force.

A log of wood is carried by the river to a lower or to a higher ground. His body, carried by the river of time, enjoys or suffers the effects of his past actions.

In the past lives, while he still dwelt in ignorance, he had created certain *karmas*. In this present life, he apparently enjoys or suffers their effects. But now he has attained illumination and no longer identifies himself with the body. His body moves among external objects and he seems to enjoy or suffer the effects of past deeds — just like a man who is still ignorant. Really, however, he is established in *Brahman*, and merely inhabits the body as a calm, detached onlooker. His mind is clear of all distraction, and unmoved, like the pivot of a wheel.

He neither directs his senses towards external objects nor does he withdraw from them. He stands like an onlooker, unconcerned. He does not desire the reward for his actions, for he is intoxicated by the *Ātman* — that nectar of pure joy.

He who renounces the pursuit of any aim, either in this world or even in the heaven itself, and remains absorbed in the *Ātman*, is indeed the Lord Śiva Himself. He is the excellent knower of *Brahman*.

Even though he dwells in the body, he is eternally free. He has reached the blessed goal. He is the excellent knower of *Brahman*. When the body falls from him he becomes merged in *Brahman*. He attains *Brahman*, the one without a second.

An actor remains the same person, even when dressed differently to play a part. The excellent knower of *Brahman* always remains *Brahman*, and nothing else.

> When an illumined soul has attained oneness with *Brahman*, his body may wither and fall anywhere, like the shrivelled leaf of a tree. What does it matter? For he has already freed himself from body-consciousness, burning it away in the fire of knowledge.
>
> The illuminated soul lives eternally conscious of his oneness with *Brahman*. He tastes continually the joy of the *Ātman*, the one without a second. In casting off this garment of skin, flesh and bone he does not have to consider if the place, the time or the circumstances are suitable.
>
> — *Vivekacūḍāmaṇi:* tr. Swami Prabhavananda and Christopher Isherwood[3]

IV

The union of *jīva* with Brahmā is eloquently described in the following Upaniṣadic passage:

3. Having entered on this path of the gods, he comes to the world of Agni, then to the world of Vāyu, then to the world of Varuṇa, then to the world of Indra, then to the world of Prajāpati, then to the world of Brahmā. This Brahmā world, verily, has the Lake Āra, the moments [spent in subduing desire, called] *yeṣṭiha*, the River Vijarā, the tree Ilya, the city Sālajya, the abode Aparājita, the two door-keepers Indra and Prajāpati, the hall Vibhu, the throne Vicakṣaṇa, the couch Amitaujas, the beloved Mānasī and her counterpart Cakṣuṣī, both of whom taking flowers, verily, weave the worlds, the mothers, the nurses, the nymphs, and the rivers. To it (to such a world) he who knows this comes. To him Brahmā runs (advances towards), and says, "It is on account of my glory, verily, he has

3. Swami Prabhavananda and Christopher Isherwood, trs., *Crest Jewel of Discrimination*, Hollywood: California: Vedanta Press, 1947, pp. 141-45.

reached the river, Ageless, He, verily, will not grow old".

4. Five hundred *apsarases* (nymphs) go towards him; one hundred with fruits in their hands, one hundred with ointments in their hands, one hundred with garlands in their hands, one hundred with powered perfumes in their hands. They adorn him with the adornment (worthy) of Brahmā. He, having been adorned with the adornment of Brahmā, goes into (advances towards) Brahmā. He comes to the Lake Āra and he crosses it with his mind. On coming to it, those who know only the immediate present, sink. He comes to the moments *yeṣṭiha* and they flee from him. He comes to the River Vijarā (Ageless); this he crosses with his mind alone. There he shakes off his good deeds and his evil deeds. His dear relatives succeed to his good deeds and those not dear, to his evil deeds. Then just as one driving a chariot, looks at the two wheels (without being touched by them), even so he will look at day and night, at good deeds and evil deeds and on all the pairs of opposites. Thus one, freed from good and freed from evil, the knower of *Brahman*, goes on to *Brahman*.

5. He comes to the tree Ilya and the fragrance of Brahmā enters into him. He comes to the city Sālajya; the flavour of Brahmā enters into him. He comes to the abode Aparājita; the radiance of Brahmā enters into him. He comes to the two door-keepers, Indra and Prajāpati and they run away from him. He comes to the hall Vibhu, and the glory of Brahmā enters into him. He comes to the throne of Vicakṣaṇa; the *Sāman* verses, *Bṛhad* and *Rathantara*, are its two forefeet, the *Śyaita* and the *Naudhasa* the two hindfeet, the *Vairūpa* and the *Vairāja*, the two lengthwise sides (pieces) the

Śākvara and the *Raivata* are the two cross ones. It is wisdom, for by wisdom, one sees clearly. He comes to the couch Amitaujas. That is the breathing spirit, the past and the future are its two forefeet, prosperity and the earth are the two hindfeet, the *Bhadra* and the *Yājñayajñīya* the two head pieces, the *Bṛhad* and the *Rathantara* the two lengthwise pieces; the *Ṛg* verses and the *Sāman* chants, the cords stretched lengthwise, the *yajus* formulas the cross ones; the moonbeams the cushion, the *udgītha* the coverlet, prosperity the pillow. On this (couch) Brahmā sits. He who knows this ascends it just with one foot only. Brahmā asks him, "Who are you?" and he should answer.

6. I am season, I am connected with the seasons. From space as the source, I am produced as the seed for a wife, as the light of the year, as the self of every single being. You are the self of every single being. What you are that am I. He says to him, "Who am I?" He should say, "The Real". What is that called the Real? Whatever is different from the gods (sense organs) and the vital breaths that is *sat*, but the gods and the vital breaths are the *tyam*. Therefore, this is expressed by the word *satyam*, all this, whatever there is. All this you are. Thus he speaks to him then. This is declared by the *Ṛg* verse.

— *Kauṣītaki-Brāhmaṇa Upaniṣad* I.3-6;
tr. S. Radhakrishnan[4]

4. S. Radhakrishnan, ed., op. cit., pp. 755-59.

15

Jñāna-Yoga

I

In order to overcome *māyā* and attain *mokṣa* one avails of a method, otherwise called *mārga* (path) or *yoga*. One such path is the path of knowledge. The most succinct statement of this is found in the statement made by Yājñavalkya to Maitreyī in the valedictory instruction before he leaves the household:

> Verily, the Self, Maitreyī, is to be seen, to be heard, to be reflected on, to be meditated upon; when verily, the Self is seen, heard, reflected on and known, then all this is known.
>
> — *Bṛhadāraṇyaka Upaniṣad* IV.5.6; tr. S. Radhakrishnan[1]

Tradition understands the statement as follows: that in order to realise *Ātman* (=*Brahman*) (1) one should hear about it (*śravaṇa*); (2) one should reflect on it (*manana*) and (3) one should meditate on it (*nididhyāsana*). Although there is difference of opinion within the tradition on their relative importance, the three elements may here be taken as indicating successive steps on the path of knowledge. The full scheme may be explained as follows:

(1) Formal study (*śravaṇa*): This signifies learning from a proper preceptor (*guru*) that the ultimate teaching of Advaita is the sole reality of *Brahman*. The unity taught here, no doubt, includes both man and nature; but as the first and foremost interest of man is man himself

1. S. Radhakrishnan, ed., *The Principal Upaniṣads*, Atlantic Heights, NJ, Humanities Press International, 1992 [1953], p. 283.

and not nature, the truth as embodied in "That thou art", or the fundamental identity of the individual and the absolute, is given prominence in the teaching. The disciple has accordingly to concentrate his attention on this aspect of the doctrine, and look upon the other, relating to nature, as more or less secondary.

(2) Reflection (*manana*): As a result of the above teaching, the disciple comes to know the unity of the individual and the ultimate reality. But this knowledge, being only communicated by another, cannot be fully convincing, especially as it is so much at variance with the verdict of common experience (*asambhāvanā*). Hence, the present step is personal reflection, which is intended to assist the disciple in convincing himself, from examples taken from ordinary life, of the correctness of Advaitic teaching. But in the very nature of the case, the arguments based on such examples are only analogical (*sāmānyato-dr̥ṣta*) for, while they are drawn from the realm of common experience, *Brahman* by hypothesis, transcends it. They can thus only give support to, or indicate the probability of, the Vedāntic truth, and cannot demonstrate it independently of revelation. In other words, this type of argument is utilised here not as a *pramāṇa* but as only an accessory to it (*yukti*). This may appear to make the Advaitic truth rest, in the end, on dogma. Such a view, however, would not be correct, as will become clear from what we shall say later regarding the place of reason in the Advaita, taken as a whole.

(3) Meditation (*dhyāna*): The object of this stage is, as often remarked before, to transform into direct experience the mediate knowledge of ultimate reality acquired by the study of the Upaniṣads and by reflection upon their teaching. It is accordingly the vision that is sought

now, and not the mere knowledge. In spite of the intellectual conviction attained, old habits of thought (*viparīta-sambhāvanā*) incompatible with it may now and again assert themselves. The present step is intended to overcome them. It consists in meditating upon the central point of the Advaitic teaching; and when that process is crowned with success, there dawns of itself upon the mind of the contemplative the truth of the statement "That thou art". The intrinsic bliss of the self also is released, as it were, in its wholeness at the same time.[2]

II

Sometimes, what one should meditate *upon* is also indicated, in case the *ātman* as such is too elusive. The following passage conjures up an archer's image, reminiscent of the association of Zen with archery.

A Target to be Penetrated by Meditation on "Oṁ"

3. Taking as a bow the great weapon of the Upaniṣad,
   One should put upon it an arrow sharpened by meditation.
   Stretching it with a thought directed to the essence of That,
   Penetrate that Imperishable as the mark, my friend.

4. The mystic syllable *oṁ* (*praṇava*) is the bow,
   The arrow is the soul (*ātman*).
   Brahma is said to be the mark (*lakṣya*).
   By the undistracted man is It to be penetrated.
   One should come to be in It, as the arrow [in the mark].

— *Muṇḍaka Upaniṣad* II.2.3-4; tr. R.E. Hume[3]

---

2. M. Hiriyanna, *The Essentials of Indian Philosophy*, pp. 171-72.
3. R.E. Hume, tr., *The Thirteen Principal Upanishads*, p. 372.

16

Bhakti-Yoga

Bhakti-yoga is already present in the Upaniṣads, indeed, *bhakti,* defined as loving devotion to God is already present in the *Ṛg-Veda,* wherein the worshipper is referred to as *deva-kāma* (desirous of god). In the Upaniṣads, the word itself appears in the *Śvetāśvatara Upaniṣad* (VI.23). However, it is in the later literature of Hinduism, such as the *Bhāgavata Purāṇa* (ninth century CE) that the path of devotion finds fuller expression. One can do no better than to cite from it, for it not merely deals with *bhakti* as such but also encompasses many different facets of the path of devotion which any student of Hinduism is bound to encounter, sooner or later.

Before the selected passages are cited, it might be useful to draw a distinction between two forms of *bhakti* (devotion): *vaidhī* and *mukhyā,* the first being formal and external and the latter internal and more real.

The external manifestations of *bhakti* in terms of form are discussed first.

I

This ninefold devotion consists of *śravaṇa* (listening); *kīrtana* (singing); *smaraṇa* (remembering); *sevana* (service); *arcana* (worship); *vandana* (prostration); *dasya* (acting as a servant); *sakhya* (befriending); and *ātmanivedana* (self-dedication). Two of these, *dāsya* and *sakhya,* overlap with several other modes of relating to God, and are discussed in the next section. These nine forms of worship are summarised in the following conversation between father and son:

> Hiraṇyakaśipu said, "Prahlāda, my child, may you live long. Tell me something of value that you have been taught by your teacher and mastered thoroughly in all these long years you have been with him." Prahlāda replied, "To hear of the glories of Viṣṇu, to praise them, to be absorbed in thoughts of Him, to wait upon Him, to worship Him, to make one's prostrations to Him, to be His dedicated servant, to look upon oneself as His friend, and to surrender oneself into His hands — if devotion to the Lord, which manifests itself in theses nine ways, were taught to the pupil, and he gave his disinterested devotion to the Lord even before he began expressing it in these various ways, that would indeed be the highest kind of learning".
>
> — *Śrīmadbhāgavatam* VII.V.19-24; tr. N. Raghunathan[1]

II

When *bhakti* becomes not merely a matter of form but a flow of loving devotion from the heart, it can take several forms, depending on how one chooses to view God: as a master, friend, father, etc. These modes are known as *bhāva*s. It is an interesting fact that even *enmity* towards God, that is, treating God as an enemy, can lead to redemption, provided it is whole-hearted. The following passage from *Śrīmadbhāgavatam* provides an example:

> Therefore, one should concentrate one's mind on the Lord so completely — either through inveterate enmity or through total freedom from it (that is, through steady and continuous devotion), or through fear, friendship or love, that he can think of nothing else. I am myself convinced that even through sustained devotion a man cannot so completely merge himself in the Lord as through inveterate enmity. The worm

1. N. Raghunathan, tr., *Śrīmadbhāgavatam*, Madras: Vighneswara Publishing House, 1976, vol. I, pp. 596-97.

immured in the wall by the wasp, thinking of it incessantly, because of the combination of hatred and fear inspiring it, is transformed into the likeness of the wasp. Likewise, those who were purified of their sins by their constant preoccupation, arising from enmity, with the exalted Lord Kṛṣṇa, the Supreme, who masqueraded as a man, attained Him. Because of their continual absorption in the Lord, either from the desire for physical union or from hatred, either from fear or friendship, many were cleansed of the sin arising from entertaining such feelings towards Him, and attained Him, as others have reached Him through loving devotion. The *gopīs* gained Him by love, Kaṁsa by fear, the King of Chedi and other rulers of men by enmity, the Vṛṣṇis by their ties of kinship, you (the Pāṇḍavas) by attachment, and we (the sages and other devotees) by devotion, my Lord. In this attitude towards the Lord, Veṇa did not behave like anyone of the five types (of those who are thus ever preoccupied with the Lord). From all this, the conclusion emerges that one should achieve mental absorption in Kṛṣṇa, through some means or other.

— *Bhāgavata Purāṇa* VII.I.21-32; with omissions; tr. N. Raghunathan[2]

III

Part (1) of this selection, deals with the path of devotion in an important school of Hindu philosophy, the Sāṁkhya. This school, which recognises matter (*prakṛti* or *pradhāna*) and spirit (*puruṣa*) as independent entities, is atheistic in its classical formulation, but ultimately developed along two lines — a theistic one as well as an atheistic one. This school is closely allied with another school of Hindu philosophy called Yoga

2. N. Raghunathan, tr., *Śrīmadbhāgavatam*, Madras: Vighneswara Publishing House, 1976, vol. I, pp. 579-80.

— to which a reference is made in part (6) as *aṣṭāṅga-yoga,* because this Yoga comprises a system with eight "limbs" or elements. Yoga accepts theism, and this may have some bearing on the development of Sāṁkhya along theistic lines. In both these systems, the first cosmic evolute from nature as a comprehensive entity called *prakṛti* or *pradhāna,* is *buddhi* or *mahat* or the organ of thinking. *Prakṛti* itself is constituted of three *guṇa*s (qualities). The word is used in a double sense: in the sense of a constituent in cosmological terms; and in the sense of a quality in individual terms. In either case they are referred to as *sattva, rajas* and *tamas.* As cosmic constituents, *sattva* stands for what is light and fine, *rajas* for energy, and *tamas* for inertia and resistance. In terms of quality, *sattva* indicates virtue, *rajas* activity, and *tamas* viciousness, or, dullness. The word is used in the second sense in part (2), in the first sense in part (6) and in both senses in part (3). The second section also uses the word *nirguṇa* not in relation to *Brahman* but *bhakti,* and *nirguṇa bhakti* was destined to become a very important concept in Hindu devotionalism.

Part (4) is important for understanding the Hindu attitude towards image-worship. Part (5) gives us some idea how the concept of hierarchy operates in *bhakti-yoga.* It is not denied, indeed, that it is systematically developed in the section, but with an egalitarian flip in the end, typical of *bhakti-yoga* which emphasises, more than *jñāna-yoga* and certainly much more than *karma-yoga,* the negligible, or at least the secondary nature of caste-distinctions. In the final section, a very different aspect of the divinity is addressed: The terrible (*raudra*) one as opposed to the gracious (*saumya*), a distinction much more clearly recognised in Śaivism and Śāktism. This section is significant in identifying its presence in Vaiṣṇavism as well.

A note about the format: There are two levels in the narration. The first level is represented by a dialogue between two sages Vidura and Maitreya. The sage is himself, however, narrating a dialogue between Devahūti and her son, Kapila, who is here considered as an incarnation of God. According to the tradition, Kapila is the founder of Sāṁkhya.

(1)

Devahūti said, "You have described the distinguishing characteristics of *mahat* and the rest, of *prakṛti* and *puruṣa*, as taught by the Sāṁkhya, so that by these characteristics one may learn their true nature. And you have also described *bhakti-yoga*, which is the fruit of such knowledge. Please tell me at length and in detail of the different ways in which that Yoga may be practised. Be pleased, also, O Lord, to describe to me the transmigratory vicissitudes to which all creatures are subject. The man who comes to know of these vicissitudes develops a distaste towards all things here and elsewhere. Please also tell me, O Lord, That art paramount over all powers, of the true nature of all-powerful time, Thy other Self, from the fear of which men live righteously. You have appeared as a veritable sun of Yoga, to awaken from their long slumber, the ignorant men plunged in the endless darkness (of *saṁsāra*), clinging on, with passionate possessiveness, to illusions (the world of phenomena) and wearied with their addiction to *karma*." (1-5)

(2)

Maitreya said: Hearing those charming words of his mother, the great sage was pleased; and applauding them, he answered her under the urge of his infinite compassion, O first of the Kurus. The Lord said: "There are many ways of practising *bhakti-yoga*, dear mother. Men's purposes differ according to their dispositions. If a man, who is irascible and dominated by the sense of difference, displays devotion to Me, whether from the desire to harm others, from hypocrisy, or from jealousy, he is a tāmasic devotee. If another, likewise, labouring under the sense of difference, worships Me in images and so on actuated by the desire for enjoyment, for fame or for sovereign power, he is a rājasic devotee. He who, while entertaining the sense of difference, worships me in order to free himself from his *karma*s, or from the desire to dedicate all work to Me, or simply from the feeling that worship is his duty, is a sāttvic devotee. The unbroken streaming of the mind towards Me, the Supreme Spirit, the Dweller in the cave of the heart — much like the flowing of the Gaṅgā waters to the sea — which starts the moment one hears My glorious qualities praised — that is the mark of the devotion that is *nirguṇa,* inspired by no ulterior end and free from notions of difference. (6-12)

(3)

Such devotees will not accept anything whatever — translation to My world, or such opulence and puissance as is Mine, close proximity to Me, assimilation to My semblance, or even absorption in My essence — should any of these things be offered to them, if it meant forgoing My service. It is this that is called the ultimate *bhakti-yoga,* which leads one beyond the sway of the three *guṇa*s to the attainment of My state (that of the Brahma). By means of the attentive and disinterested practice of one's own duties; by the devout and steady performance of My worship with no hankering for the fruits thereof, and without causing any injury or serious inconvenience to others; by gazing with reverence on My image or on any other vehicle in which I am invoked, lovingly touching it, offering worship with the singing of hymns and the making of prostrations; learning to look on Me as present in all creatures; cultivating courage and detachment; showing great respect to the saintly, sympathy to the lowly, and friendship to one's equals;

practising the internal and external disciplines; listening to the exposition of the Śāstra that teaches discrimination between the Self and the non-Self; devoutly reciting My names; cultivating perfect sincerity and straightforwardness; consorting with the virtuous, and abjuring the attitude of possessiveness — by these means, the mind of the man, who devotes himself to the *dharma* that leads to Me, is purified, and it turns to Me the moment it hears My praises sung. Just as the fragrance, that is carried by the air from its source, takes possession of the sense of smell, so does the mind, devoted to Yoga and steadied by it, appropriate Me, the *paramātman.* (13-20)

(4)

I am ever present in all creatures as the Inner Ruler. He who treats Me with contempt there, while pretending to worship Me in an image, makes a farce of worship. He who ignores My presence in all creatures as their Soul and Inner Ruler, and in his folly worships an image, is like one who makes oblations in ashes. The mind of that man can never know peace, who labours under the sense of difference and is so much in love with himself that he develops inveterate hostility to all creatures, and thus hates Me, since I am present in all of them. The man who condemns all creatures, can never hope to propitiate Me, the flawless one, however opulent the worship he might offer Me in an image. (21-24)

So long as man does not realise Me in the core of his heart, Me, the Dweller in all hearts, he should worship Me, the Supreme Lord, in images and the like, while scrupulously discharging his duties. To the man who discriminates between himself and another, on the ground of their separate hungers, I come as Death, and I inflict on him the dreaded travail of *saṁsāra*. Therefore, while maintaining an equable attitude towards all creatures, men should worship Me suitably in all of them, since I abide in them as the Inner Ruler, by making them gifts, rendering them due honour, or giving them their friendship, as might seem proper. (25-27)

(5)

Living things are superior to those that are inanimate. Higher than the former are the creatures that draw breath, O auspicious dame; greater than these are those that are endowed with consciousness; higher than these are those whose organs of sensation are active. Among those endowed with different senses — touch, taste, smell, hearing and the capacity to distinguish colours — superiority obtains in that order. Those that have two rows of teeth are better than those that have only one. Those that have many feet are better than those that have none. Superior to the former are those that have only four; and even higher are those that have only two. Among the bipeds, those who belong to the four *varṇa*s, are superior to the rest; and among these the highest is the brāhmaṇa. Among brāhmaṇas, the man who has learnt the Vedas is superior to others; superior to him is the man who knows the meaning of the Veda. Higher than him is the man who can help clarify doubts. Better than him is the man who is faithful to his *dharma*. Far superior to him is the man who has given up all attachments, and has renounced the fruits of *dharma*. Even greater than he is the man who dedicates all actions, and their fruits, and his body (and all other possessions) to Me; so nothing divides him from Me. I can, in fact, think of none who is superior to him, who has put himself into My hands and renounced all fruits of action in My favour, who makes no difference between creature and creature and has ceased to entertain the egoistic notion that he is the doer. One must mentally offer one's utmost reverence to all creatures, remembering that the Supreme Lord is there in them, as the Controller of the *jīva*. (28-34)

(6)

I have now explained to you at length, O daughter of Manu, *bhakti-yoga*, as well as *aṣṭāṅga-yoga*. By either of these means one may attain the Supreme Lord. It is this form of the Lord, Who is the Brahmā and the *paramātman*, and Who stands forth as the *pradhāna* and the *puruṣa*, and as That Which is different from and beyond them both, that is called *daiva* (Destiny), since it causes the infinite diversity of the transmigratory existence, by prompting the doing of actions (by the *jīva*s). This form of the Lord is also known as time, which is the cause of the changes that all things undergo. Its power is marvellous, and it inspires terror in all *jīva*s, beginning with that which animates the *mahat*, since they are obsessed by the notion of difference. Time, which enters into all creatures as their sustainer, destroys them through the instrumentality of other creatures, and is paramount over all, including those who (like Brahmā), have absolute power over all creatures. For, it is none other than the Lord, Who is known as Viṣṇu, the Abode of all creatures, and the Dispenser of the fruits of the sacrifice. To the Lord, Who functions as time, no one is dear; He looks upon none as His enemy or as His kin. Ever vigilant, He, their death, enters into those who are heedless of their own lasting good. It is from fear of Him that the wind blows, the sun shines, the god (Indra) sends down showers, and the hosts of luminaries shed light; from fear of Him the trees, the creepers and the annuals yield fruit and flower in their season. The rivers run from fear of Him. And it is from fear of Him that the sea does not overflow its bounds, that fire burns, and the earth, with its mountains, does not sink into the waters. It is by His command that space contains all living beings and the *mahat* expands itself into the cosmos enveloped by its seven covers. It is from fear of Him that the gods, who preside over the three *guṇa*s, and to whose will this universe of the stationary and the moving is subject, set about their work-creation, and so on — again and again. While He as time is the Creator, bringing about the generation of creatures by other creatures, and is also the Destroyer, Who inflicts death on Death itself, He himself knows neither beginning nor end, neither change nor decay. (35-45)

— *Bhāgavata Purāṇa*, III.29; tr. N. Raghunathan[3]

3. N. Raghunathan, tr., *Śrīmadbhāgavatam*, Madras: Vighneswara Publishing House, 1976, vol. I, pp. 247-51. Diacritics added, some words italicized.

17

Karma-Yoga

Just as the early Upaniṣads constitute a major source regarding the path of knowledge and just as the *Bhāgavata Purāṇa* is a venerable source regarding the path of devotion; the *Bhagavad-Gītā* serves as a standard guidebook for the path of action. This should not mislead one into believing that these three sources expound only *jñāna-yoga*, *bhakti-yoga* and *karma-yoga* to the exclusion of the others. The textual reality is more complex. However, it is nevertheless true that they have come to be strongly associated with those particular *yogas*, notwithstanding their broader sweep.

I

Perhaps, the setting of the *Bhagavad-Gītā* has played a major role in establishing it as virtually a gospel of *karma-yoga*. It starts with Arjuna, a warrior, on the point of abandoning his position on the battlefield and expressing preference for leading a life of renunciation rather than action. Ultimately, he is convinced by his friend and charioteer, Kṛṣṇa, who is also regarded as an incarnation, to resume the struggle. One of the arguments which, at least initially, Kṛṣṇa uses to persuade Arjuna to fight is to remind him that he is a kṣatriya (a warrior) and it is his duty to fight. In the last chapter, Kṛṣṇa presents a more broad-based argument, which entails the performance of duty on the part of all the four *varṇa*s: brāhmaṇa (priests); kṣatriya (warriors); vaiśya (commoners) and śūdra (servants):

41. The action of priests, warriors, commoners, and servants are apportioned by qualities born of their intrinsic being.

42. Tranquillity, control, penance, purity, patience and honesty, knowledge, judgement, and piety are intrinsic to the action of a priest.

43. Heroism, fiery energy, resolve, skill, refusal to retreat in battle, charity, and majesty in conduct are intrinsic to the action of a warrior.

44. Farming, herding cattle, and commerce are intrinsic to the action of a commoner; action that is essentially service is intrinsic to the servant.

45. Each one achieves success by focusing on his own action; hear how one finds success by focusing on his own action.

46. By his own action a man finds success, worshipping the source of all creatures' activity, the presence pervading all that is.

47. Better to do one's own duty imperfectly than to do another man's well; doing action intrinsic to his being, a man avoids guilt.

48. Arjuna, a man should not relinquish action he is born to, even if it is flawed; all undertakings are marred by a flaw, as fire is obscured by smoke.

49. His understanding everywhere detached, the self mastered, longing gone, one finds through renunciation the supreme success beyond action.

50. Understand in summary from me how when he achieves success one attains the infinite spirit, the highest state of knowledge.

51. Armed with his purified understanding, subduing the

self with resolve, relinquishing sensuous objects, avoiding attraction and hatred;

52. Observing solitude, barely eating, restraining speech, body, and mind; practising discipline in meditation, cultivating dispassion;

53. Freeing himself from individuality, force, pride, desire, anger, acquisitiveness; unpossessive, tranquil, he is at one with the infinite spirit.

54. Being at one with the infinite spirit serene in himself, he does not grieve or crave; impartial toward all creatures, he achieves supreme devotion to me.

55. Through devotion he discerns me, just who and how vast I really am; and knowing me in reality, he enters into my presence.

56. Always performing all actions, taking refuge in me, he attains through my grace the eternal place beyond change.

57. Through reason, renounce all work in me, focus on me; relying on the discipline of understanding, always keep me in your thought.

58. If I am in your thought, by my grace you will transcend all dangers; but if you are deafened by individuality, you will be lost.

59. Your resolve is futile if a sense of individuality makes you think, "I shall not fight" — nature will compel you to.

60. You are bound by your own action, intrinsic to your being, Arjuna; even against your will you must do what delusion now makes you refuse.

61. Arjuna, the lord resides in the heart of all creatures, making them reel magically, as if a machine moved them.

62. With your whole being, Arjuna take refuge in him alone — from his grace you will attain the eternal place that is peace.

— *Bhagavad-Gītā* XVIII.41-62; tr. Barbara Stoler Miller.[1]

Certain points deserve attention. First, it is pointed out to Arjuna that no form of action (inaction also being a form of action) is free from taint. Second, that if one performs an action different from the one intrinsic to one's being, one will get into greater difficulties, hence even if another's action appears superior to one's own, but is not intrinsic to one's nature, one's own action remains superior to it. Third, what does doing one's duty imperfectly mean? In the context of the *Gītā*, an action is imperfect if it is performed for the sake of its fruits and not for its own sake. To seek a reward for one's duty means that one's duty will never be its own reward — this is what makes it imperfect. But even such action performed imperfectly is better than another's duty performed well? How could this be so? This is because what counts is not *what* is done but *how* it is done. And *how* it is done is not a matter of how well it is done in *form* but how it is performed in *spirit*. Another's duty, because it is artificial, cannot be performed naturally in such a way that it is a complete act in itself, without any consideration of its results. Such abandonment of the fruit of action is difficult even in the case of actions intrinsic to one's being, but in such case it is at least possible, if difficult. It is just not possible in the other case.

To break this inveterate connection between action and the desire for its fruit, the *Gītā* suggests several techniques, involving simple preaching as well as subtler teachings.

The passage cited earlier suggests how renunciation of the *fruit* of action rather than of action, or renunciation in

1. Barbara Stoler Miller, *The Bhagavadgītā: Kṛṣṇa's Counsel in Time of War*, New York: Columbia University Press, 1986, pp. 149-55. Verses 41-42 were cited earlier in chapter 12, in another translation.

action, as some have put it, may be achieved. It may be achieved by eliminating desire itself — the absolutistic route; or merging one's own will with God's will — the theistic root. Either way, the path of action will lead to liberation.

II

Although the path of action, as prescribed in the *Gītā*, has achieved the status of becoming virtually canonical, in some texts the path of action is said to lead to liberation in a somewhat different way. This optional way seems to operate on an improved version of the maxim: nothing succeeds like success, namely nothing succeeds like excess — for it generates detachment, which is the crucial turning-point on the road to liberation.

> Those who are enlightened by the Veda consider that the *dharma*s prescribed for men in every *yuga* are those that are mostly determined by their own disposition. These, if followed faithfully, will bring them nothing but good here and hereafter. The man who, discharging the duties incumbent on him, adopts the means of livelihood that has been prescribed as most in accord with his natural disposition, comes gradually to be freed from bondage to the *karma*s determined by his nature, and thus, from the sway of the *guṇa*s. The field that is sown again and again becomes barren; it loses its capacity to produce, and the seed sown in it perishes. Likewise, the mind, which is the storehouse of latent desires, develops a distaste for pleasures from excessive addiction, O king, not from small indulgences; even as fire is not put out by drops of ghee (which a copious draught would put out).
>
> — *Bhāgavata Purāṇa* VI.11.30-355;
> with some omissions, tr. N. Raghunathan[2]

2. N. Raghunathan, tr., *Śrīmadbhāgavatam*, p. 632.

III

The doctrine of *karma* should not be confused with that of *karma-yoga*. *Karma-yoga* is the antidote of *karma*.

> As I thus listened regularly, thrice a day, throughout the rainy season and the autumn, to the immaculate glory of Hari, sung by the high-souled sages, there grew in my heart the devotion that frees one from *rajas* and *tamas*. When I had thus been cleansed of my sins, and they found me loving, humble and attentive as well as self-controlled and dutiful in their service, though still a child, they, who loved the lowly, taught me out of their abundant kindness, when they were about to leave, the extremely secret Śāstra (the *Bhāgavatam*) which the Lord Himself had revealed. Through that Śāstra I became aware of the mighty power of *māyā* of the exalted Lord Vāsudeva, the Creator, by gaining knowledge of which men reach His abode. And, it was broadly indicated to me, O *Brahman*, that the cure for the three kinds of ills was the dedication of all *karma*s to the exalted and Paramount Lord, Who is eternally perfect. A substance that breeds disease in living creatures will not, O you of the steadfast vows, effect a cure thereof, if used as it is. But, if it is suitably medicated, it does. Even thus, while all *karma*s lead into involvement in *saṁsāra*, they are annulled when they are dedicated to the Transcendent Lord (28-34).'
>
> — *Bhāgavata Purāṇa* I.V.28-34;
> tr. N. Raghunathan, Emphasis added[3]

3. N. Raghunathan, tr., op. cit., p. 18.

18

Varṇa

One of the key organising concepts in Hinduism, in relation to society, is that of *varṇa*. From the classical period of Hinduism onwards, the key dimension of this concept of *varṇa* is the relationship it exhibits to that of *jāti*, a related concept from which it must be carefully distinguished.

The *varṇa*s are regularly described as four in number — comprising the four social classes, usually specified as consisting of the brāhmaṇa (priests, etc.); kṣatriya (warriors, etc.); vaiśya (merchants, etc.) and śūdra (servants, etc.). The *jāti*s, on the other hand, are undetermined in number. During the classical period, Hindu society witnessed the rise of a number of *jāti*s, that is, of endogamous, commensal and often craft-exclusive groups, which shared these features broadly with the *varṇa*s qualitatively, but were typically smaller in size, and were often subsumed under the *varṇa*s. Just to give an idea, it has been assessed that anywhere from one to ten thousand *jāti*s may have thus been encompassed within the four *varṇa*s, at various points in time.

Many scholars are of the view that, in the classical period of Hinduism, the four *varṇa*s, which may originally have been constituted as a vocational classification with a large measure of flexibility, became associated with *jāti*s, and therefore, became more rigid in character, though never quite losing their flexible character. This phenomenon could be described as the *jātification* of the *varṇa* system, when natal determination becomes a prominent feature of Hindu social thought in this period.

The so-called caste system of Hinduism represents a kind

of coming together of the concepts of *varṇa* and *jāti*, as represented in the *Manusmṛti*, an authoritative Hindu law book often assigned to the second century.

It is, however, important to distinguish between these two:

> Most of the misunderstanding on the subject has arisen from the persistent mistranslation of Manu's term *varṇa* as "caste", whereas it should be rendered "class" or "order", or by some equivalent term.
>
> The compiler of the *Institutes of Manu* was well aware of the distinction between *varṇa* and *jāti*. While he mentions about 50 different castes, he lays much stress on the fact that there are only four *varṇa*s. The two terms are carelessly confused in one particular passage (X.31), but in that only. Separate castes existed from an early date. Their relations to one another remaining unaffected whether they are grouped theoretically under four occupational headings or not.[1]

The foregoing explanation was necessary to account for the logic of the selections in this section. The various selections highlight the dissonance in the social system on account of the absence of a neat fit between the *varṇa* and *jāti* concepts. Two points of significance surface in this context: (1) If the natal determination of *jāti* is taken for granted, and it is then brought in relation to *varṇa*, the question naturally arises: is *varṇa* based on birth, too, like the *jāti*? Although this has often been assumed, it was not an assumption which went unquestioned. The point is illustrated by a selection from the *Mahābhārata*. (2) In view of this lack of perfect fit between *varṇa* and *jāti*, the question also naturally arises whether this fact also translated into a discrepancy between law and practice in the social life of classical Hinduism. This is where the accounts of foreign observers become relevant, for what they report may

1. Percival Spear, ed., *The Oxford History of India* (4th edn.), Delhi: Oxford University Press, 1981, pp. 63-64.

represent a reality, not revealed by the limited lenses of the standard texts. This point is illustrated by the selections from Greek and Muslim accounts. These accounts also indicate the vast changes the system had undergone, and how anthropological, as opposed to classical textual, perceptions may differ in this respect.

I

The following dialogue between King Nahuṣa, in the form of a snake, and Yudhiṣṭhira, occurs in the *Mahābhārata*:

> *The snake said:*
>
> Now, who is brāhmaṇa, king, and what may he know, Yudhiṣṭhira? Speak up, for from your words we gather that you are very wise!
>
> *Yudhiṣṭhira said:*
>
> He is known as a brāhmaṇa, king of snakes, in whom truthfulness, liberality, patience, deportment, mildness, self-control, and compassion are found. And he may gain knowledge of the Supreme *Brahman*, beyond happiness and unhappiness, snake, on reaching which they grieve no more. What more do you wish to say?
>
> *The snake said:*
>
> Authority, truth, and the *Brahman* extend to all four classes: even śūdras may be truthful, liberal, tolerant, mild, non-violent, and compassionate, Yudhiṣṭhira. The object of knowledge, you say, king of men, is beyond happiness and unhappiness; but not a thing is free from either, and I do not think it exists.
>
> *Yudhiṣṭhira said:*
>
> The marks of the śūdra are not found in a brāhmaṇa; but a śūdra is not necessarily a śūdra, nor a brāhmaṇa a brāhmaṇa. In whomever the brāhmaṇa's marks are found, snake, he is known as a brāhmaṇa; and in whom they are not found, him they designate as a śūdra.

However, if you proclaim that this object of knowledge does not exist, since there is not a thing here that is free from either happiness or unhappiness, that is your opinion, snake, that there is nothing free from either. Just as in between cold and heat there is neither cold nor heat, so there can be something somewhere in which there is neither happiness nor unhappiness: this is my view, snake, or what do you think?

The snake said:

If you judge a brāhmaṇa by his conduct, king, then birth has no meaning, my dear sir, as long as no conduct is evident.

Yudhiṣṭhira said:

I think, great and wise serpent, that birth is hard to ascertain among humankind, because of the confusion of all classes when any man begets children by any woman: language, intercourse, birth and death are the common lot of all men. The standard of the seers is expressed in the formula *ye yajāmahe*, "We, such as we are, give worship". Therefore, those see the truth of it who know that conduct is the chief postulate. It is enjoined that the birth rite takes place before the navel string is cut; the Sāvatrī formula is called the mother there, and the teacher the father. One is reckoned the same, as a śūdra by conduct, as long as one is not reborn in the Veda. In the difference of opinion on this Manu Svayaṁbhuva has said decisively, "Class is determined by observance of tasks. If no conduct is observed, there is judged to be an overwhelming class mixture", O Indra of snakes.[2]

II

The Greek accounts go as far back as the fourth century BCE. The one included here, has come down from the first century BCE. It is by Megasthenês and is significant inasmuch as towards

2. J.A.B. van Buitenen, tr., *The Mahābhārata*, Chicago and London: Chicago University Press, 1975, vol. II, p. 564.

the end it alludes to endogamy and craft-exclusiveness, which were destined to become such dominant features of the system of castes among the Indians.

> (39) According to him (Megasthenês), the population of India is divided into seven [parts]. The philosophers are first in rank, but form the smallest class in point of number. Their services are employed [privately] by persons who wish to offer sacrifices or [perform other sacred rites,] and also [publicly] by the kings at what is called the Great Synod, wherein, at the beginning of the new year, all the philosophers, are gathered together before the king at the gates, when any philosopher, who may have committed any useful suggestion to writing texts, or observed any means for [improving the crops and the cattle, or for promoting the public interests,] declares it publicly. If anyone is detected giving false information thrice, the law condemns him to be silent for the rest of his life, but he who [gives sound advice] is exempted from paying any taxes or contributions.
>
> (40) The *second* caste consists of the husbandmen, who form the bulk of the population, and are in disposition most mild and gentle. They are exempted from military service, and cultivate their lands undisturbed by fear. They never go to town, either to take part in its tumults, or for any other purpose. It therefore, not infrequently happens, that at the same time, and in the same part of the country, men may be seen drawn up in an array of battle, and fighting at the risk of their lives, while other men *close at hand*, are ploughing and digging in *perfect* security; having these soldiers to protect them. The whole of the land is the property of the king, and the husbandmen till it [on condition of receiving one-fourth of the produce.]
>
> (41) The *third* caste consists of herdsmen and hunters, who alone are allowed to hunt, and to [keep] cattle, and to sell drought animals or let them out on hire. In

return for clearing the land of wild beasts and fowls, which devour the seeds sown in the fields, they receive an allowance of grain from the king. They lead a wandering life and live under tents.

Fragm. XXXVI. follows here.

[So much, then, on the subject of wild animals. We shall now return to Megasthenês, and resume from where we disgressed.]

(46) The *fourth* class, after herdsmen and hunters, consists of those who work at trades, of those who vend wares, and of those who are employed in bodily labour. Some of these pay tribute, and render to the state certain prescribed services. But the armour-makers and the shipbuilders receive wages and [their victuals] from the king, for whom alone they work. The general in command of the army supplies the soldiers with weapons, and the admiral of the fleet lets out ships on hire [for the transport both of passengers and merchandise].

(47) The *fifth* class consists of fightingmen, who, when not engaged in active service, pass their time in idleness and drinking. They are maintained at the king's expense, and hence, they are always ready, whenever occasion calls, to take the field, for they carry nothing of their own with them but their own bodies.

(48) The *sixth* class consists of the overseers, to whom is assigned the duty of watching all that goes on, and making reports secretly to the king. Some are entrusted with the inspection of the city, and others with that of the army. The former employ as their coadjutors, the courtesans of the city, and the latter the courtesans of the camp. The ablest and the most trustworthy men are appointed to fill these offices.

The *seventh* class consists of [the councillors and assessors] of the king. To them belong the highest posts of government, the tribunals of justice, and the general

> administration of public affairs. No one is allowed to marry out of his own caste, or to exchange one profession or trade for another, or to follow more than one business. An exception is made in favour of the philosopher, who for his virtue, is allowed this privilege.
>
> — Megasthenês, as redacted by Strabo; tr. J.W. McCrindle[3]

The last few sentences above are elaborated as follows by Arrian:

> The custom of the country prohibits inter-marriage between the castes: for instance, the husbandmen cannot take a wife from the artisan caste, nor the artisan a wife from the husbandman caste. Custom also prohibits anyone from exercising two trades, or from changing from one caste to another. One cannot, for instance, become a husbandman if he is a herdsman, or become a herdsman if he is an artisan. It is permitted that the sophist only be from any caste: for the life of the sophist is not an easy one, but the hardest of all.
>
> — Arrian XI-XII; tr. J.W. McCrindle, emphasis added[4]

III

The account by Albiruni (973-1048) demonstrates the changes the *varṇa* system had undergone over the years. Megasthenês does not even mention the word but Albiruni provides a detailed account in Chapter IX of his work, made famous under the title *Alberuni's India* by its translator.

On the Castes, Called "Colours" (*varṇa*), and on The Classes Below Them

> If a new order of things in political or social life is created by a man naturally ambitious of ruling, who

3. J.W. McCrindle, *Ancient India as Described by Megasthenês and Arrian* (revised 2nd edn. by R.C. Majumdar), Calcutta: Chuckervertty Chatterjee & Co., 1960, pp. 83-86.
4. Ibid., pp. 214-18.

by his character and capacity really deserves to be a ruler, a man of firm convictions and unshaken determination, who even in times of reverses is supported by good luck, in so far as people, then side with him in recognition of the former merits of his; such an order is likely to become consolidated among those for whom it was created, and continue to be as firm as the deeply rooted mountains. It will remain among them as a generally recognised rule, in all generations through the course of time and the flight of ages. If, then, this new form of state or society rests in some degree on religion, these twins, state and religion, are in perfect harmony, and their union represents the highest development of human society, all that men can possibly desire.

The kings of antiquity, who were industriously devoted to the duties of their office, spent most of their care on the division of their subjects into different classes and orders, which they tried to preserve from intermixture and disorder. Therefore, they forbade people of different classes to have intercourse with each other, and laid upon each class a particular kind of work or art and handicraft. They did not allow anybody to transgress the limits of his class, and even punished those who would not be content with their class.

All this is well illustrated by the history of the ancient Chosroes (Khusrau), for they had created great instructions of their kind, which could not be broken through by the special merits of any individual nor by bribery. When Ardashīr ben Bābak restored the Persian empire, he also restored the classes or castes of the population in the following way:

> "*The first class* were the knights and princes.
> *The second class* the monks, the fire-priests, and the lawyers.

The third class the physicians, astronomers, and other men of science."

And within these classes there were subdivisions, distinct from each other, like the species within a genus. All institutions of this kind are like a pedigree, as long as their origin is remembered; but when once their origin has been forgotten, they become, as it were, the stable property of the whole nation, nobody any more questioning its origin. And forgetting is the necessary result of any long period of time, of a long succession of centuries and generations.

Among the Hindus, institutions of this kind abound. We Muslims, of course, stand entirely on the other side of the question, considering all men as equal, except in piety; and this is the greatest obstacle which prevents any approach or understanding between Hindus and Muslims.

Then Hindus call their caste *varṇa*, i.e. *colours*, and from a genealogical point of view they call them *jātaka*, i.e. *births*. These castes are from the very beginning only four.

I. The highest caste is the brāhmaṇa, of whom the books of the Hindus tell that they were created from the head of *Brahman*. And as *Brahman* is only another name for the force called *nature*, and the head is the highest part of the animal body, the brāhmaṇas are the choice part of the whole genus, therefore the Hindus consider them as the very best of mankind.

II. The next caste is the kṣatriya, who were created, as they say, from the shoulders and hands of *Brahman*. Their degree is not much below that of the brāhmaṇa.

III. After them follow the vaiśya, who were created from the thigh of *Brahman*.

IV. The śūdra, who were created from his feet.

Between the latter two classes there is no very great distance. Much, however, as these classes differ from each other, they live together in the same towns and villages, mixed together in the same houses and lodgings.

After the śūdra follow the people called *antyaja*, who render various kinds of services, who are not reckoned amongst any caste, but only as members of a certain craft or profession. There are eight classes of them, who freely intermarry with each other, except the fuller, shoemaker, and weaver, for no others would condescend to have anything to do with them. These eight guilds are the fuller, shoemaker, juggler, the basket and shield maker, the sailor, fisherman, the hunter of wild animals and of birds, and the weaver. The four castes do not live together with them in one and the same place. These guilds live near the villages and towns of the four castes, but outside them.

The people called Hāḍī, Ḍoma (Ḍomba), Caṇḍāla, and Badhatau (*sic*) are not reckoned amongst any caste or guild. They are occupied with dirty work, like the cleansing of villages and other services. They are considered as one sole class, and distinguished only by their occupations. In fact, they are considered like illegitimate children; for according to general opinion they descend from a śūdra father and a brāhmaṇa mother as the children of fornication; therefore they are degraded outcasts.

The Hindus give to every single man of the four castes characteristic names, according to their occupations and modes of life, e.g. the brāhmaṇa is in general called by his name as long as he does work staying at home. When he is busy with the service of one fire, he is called *iṣṭin;* if he serves three fires, he is called *agnihôtrin*; if he besides offers an offering to the fire, he is called *dīkṣita*. And as it is with the brāhmaṇa, so is it also with the other castes. Of the classes *beneath* the castes, the Hāḍī are the best spoken of, because they keep themselves free from everything unclean. Next follow the Ḍoma, who play on the lute and sing. The still lower classes practise as a trade killing and the inflicting of judicial punishments. The worst of all are the Badhatau, who not only devour the flesh of dead animals, but even of dogs and other beasts.

Each of the four castes, when eating together, must form a group for themselves, one group not being allowed to comprise two men of different castes. If, further, in the group of the brāhmaṇa there are two men who live at enmity with each other, and the seat of the one is by the side of the other, they make a barrier between the two seats by placing a board between them, or by spreading a piece of dress, or in some other way; and if there is only a line drawn between them, they are considered as separated. Since it is forbidden to eat the remains of a meal, every single man must have his own food for himself; for anyone of the party who are eating should take of the food from one and the same plate, that which remains in the plate becomes, after the first eater has taken part, to him who wants to take as the second, *the remains of the meal*, and such is forbidden.

Hindus differ among themselves as to which of these castes is capable of attaining to liberation; for, according to some, only the brāhmaṇa and kṣatriya are capable of it, since the others cannot learn the Veda, whilst according to the Hindu philosophers, liberation is common to all castes and to the whole human race, if their intention of obtaining it is perfect. This view is based on the saying of Vyāsa: "Learn to know the twenty-five things thoroughly. Then you may follow whatever religion you like; you will no doubt be liberated." This view is also based on the fact that Vāsudeva was a descendant of a śūdra family, and also on the following saying of his, which he addressed to Arjuna: "God distributes recompense without injustice and without partiality. He reckons the good as bad if people in doing good forget him; he reckons the bad as good if people doing bad remember him and do not forget him, whether those people be vaiśya or śūdra or women. How much more will this be the case when they are brāhmaṇa or kṣatriya."[5]

5. Ainslie T. Embree, ed., *Alberuni's India*; translated by Edward C. Sachau, New York: W.W. Norton & Company, 1971, part I, pp. 99-104.

19

Āśrama

In its classical conception, one is supposed to pass through each of the *āśramas*: of the student, householder, hermit and renunciant — in that order. This passage through the *āśramas* is confined to the male members of the three higher *varṇas* (brāhmaṇa, kṣatriya, vaiśya) according to most of the law-books of classical Hinduism, although there is some evidence suggestive of more concessive stance towards women and the śūdras in practice (see P.V. Kane, *History of Dharmaśāstra*, Poona: Bhandarkar Oriental Research Institute, 1974, vol. II, Part II, pp. 944-45). We begin with an account of the life of the student. Our source is the *Manusmṛti*, considered the most authoritative among the texts of the genre.

I

The rules for the life of the student pertain to his initiation and to his subsequent conduct as a student. The initiation involves the chanting of the mystic *oṁ* along with the initiatory verse: *Ṛg-Veda* III.63.10: "We meditate on the excellent light of the divine sun; may he illumine our minds" (Wilson's translation).

The initiation is followed by a life led as celibate student, for which numerous edifying rules are laid down. Some of which are included in the selection below:

II.68. Thus has been described the rule for the initiation of the twice-born, which indicates a (new) birth, and sanctifies; learn (now) to what duties they must afterwards apply themselves.

69. Having performed the (rite of) initiation, the teacher must first instruct the (pupil) in (the rules of) personal purification, of conduct, of the fire-worship, and of the twilight devotions.

70. But (a student) who is about to begin the study (of the Veda), shall receive instruction, after he has sipped water in accordance with the institutes (of the sacred law); has made the *brahmāñjali*, (has put on) a clean dress, and has brought his organs under the control.

71. At the beginning and at the end of (a lesson in the) Veda he must always clasp both the feet of his teacher, (and) he must study, joining his hands; that is called the *brahmāñjali* (joining the palms for the sake of the Veda).

72. With crossed hands he must clasp (the feet) of the teacher, and touch the left (foot) with his left (hand), the right (foot) with his right (hand).

73. But to him who is about to begin studying, the teacher, always unwearied, must say: Ho, recite! He shall leave off (when the teacher says): Let a stoppage take place!

74. Let him always pronounce the syllable *oṁ* at the beginning and at the end of (a lesson in) the Veda; (for) unless the syllable *oṁ* precede (the lesson) will slip away (from him), and unless it follow it will fade away.

75. Seated on (blades of *kuśa* grass), and sanctified by three suppressions of the breath (*prāṇāyāma*), he is worthy (to pronounce) the syllable *oṁ*.

76. Prajāpati (the lord of creatures), milked out (as it were) from the three Vedas the sounds A, U, and Ṁ, and (the *vyāhr̥tis*) *bhūḥ, bhuvaḥ, svaḥ*.

77. Moreover, from the three Vedas, Prajāpati, who dwells in the highest heaven (*parameṣṭhin*), milked out (as it were) the *R̥k*-verse, sacred to Savitr̥ (Sāvitrī), which begins with the word tad, one foot from each.

78. A Brāhmaṇa, learned in the Veda, who recites during both twilights that syllable and that (verse), preceded by the *vyāhṛtis*, gains the (whole) merit which (the recitation of) the Vedas confers.

79. A twice-born man who (daily) repeats those three one thousand times outside (the village), will be freed after a month even from great guilt, as a snake from its slough.

80. The Brāhmaṇa, the Kṣatriya, and the Vaiśya who neglect (the recitation of) that *Ṛk*-verse and the timely (performance of the) rites (prescribed for them) will be blamed among virtuous men.

86. The four *pākayajña*s and those sacrifices which are enjoined by the rules (of the Veda) are all together not equal in value to a sixteenth part of the sacrifice consisting of muttered prayers.

87. But, undoubtedly, a Brāhmaṇa reaches the highest goal by muttering prayers only; (whether) he performs other (rites) or neglects them, he who befriends (all creatures) is declared (to be) a (true) Brāhmaṇa.

88. A wise man should strive to restrain his organs, which run wild among alluring sensual objects, like a charioteer his horses.

89. Those eleven organs which former sages have named, I will properly (and) precisely enumerate in due order,

90. (Viz.) the ear, the skin, the eyes, the tongue, and the nose as the fifth, the anus, the organ of generation, hands and feet, and the (organ of) speech, named as the tenth.

91. Five of them, the ear and the rest, according to their order, they call organs of sense, and five of them, the anus and the rest, organs of action.

92. Know that the internal organ (*manas*) is the eleventh, which by its quality belongs to both (sets); when that has been subdued, both those sets of five have been conquered.

93. Through the attachment of his organs (to sensual pleasure) a man doubtlessly will incur guilt; but if he keeps them under complete control, he will obtain success (in gaining all his aims).

94. Desire is never extinguished by the enjoyment of desired objects; it only grows stronger like a fire (fed) with clarified butter.

95. If one man should obtain all those (sensual enjoyments) and another should renounce them all, the renunciation of all pleasures is far better than the attainment of them.

154. Let him reverentially salute venerable men (who visit him), give them his own seat, let him sit near them with joined hands and, when they leave, (accompany them), walking behind them.

155. Let him, untired, follow the conduct of virtuous men, connected with his occupations, which has been fully declared in the revealed texts and in the sacred tradition (Smṛti) and is the root of the sacred law.

156. Through virtuous conduct he obtains long life, through virtuous conduct desirable offspring, through virtuous conduct imperishable wealth; virtuous conduct destroys (the effect of) inauspicious marks.

157. For a man of bad conduct is blamed among people, (he) constantly suffers misfortunes, is afflicted with diseases, and (is) short-lived.

158. A man who follows the conduct of the virtuous, has faith and is free from envy, lives a hundred years, though he be entirely destitute of auspicious marks.

159. Let him carefully avoid all undertakings (the success of) which depends on others; but let him eagerly pursue that (the accomplishment of) which depends on himself.

160. Everything that depends on others (gives) pain, everything that depends on oneself (gives) pleasure; know that this is the short definition of pleasure and pain.

161. When the performance of an act gladdens his heart, let him perform it with diligence; but let him avoid the opposite.

162. Let him never offend the teacher who initiated him, nor him who explained the Veda, nor his father and mother, nor (any other) Guru, nor cows, nor Brāhmaṇas, nor any men performing austerities.

163. Let him avoid atheism, cavilling at the Vedas, contempt of the gods, hatred, want of modesty, pride, anger, and harshness.

164. Let him, when angry, not raise a stick against another man, nor strike (anybody) except a son or pupil; those two he may beat in order to correct them.

170. Neither a man who (lives) unrighteously, nor he who (acquires) wealth (by telling) falsehoods, nor he who always delights in doing injury, ever attains happiness in this world.

171. Let him, though suffering in consequence of his righteousness, never turn his heart to unrighteousness; for he will see the speedy overthrow of unrighteous, wicked men.

172. Unrighteousness, practised in this world, does not at once produce its fruit, like a cow; but, advancing slowly, it cuts off the roots of him who committed it.

— *Manusmṛti* II.68-80; 86-95; IV. 154-64; 170-72; tr. G. Bühler[1]

1. G. Bühler, tr., op. cit., pp. 42-47; 58-61.

II

The rules of the life of the householder are laid down as follows. Some of the duties are ritually complex, only the simple but important rules are noted here. The last verse contains a reference to the *pañca-mahāyajña*s or the five great sacrifices meant to be performed daily by the householder: (1) studying the Veda; (2) sacrificing to the gods; (3) offering oblations to ancestors; (4) hospitality to guests, and (5) offering food to living beings.

1. The vow (of studying) the three Vedas under a teacher must be kept for thirty-six years, or for half that time, or for a quarter, or until the (student) has perfectly learnt them.

2. (A student) who has studied in due order the three Vedas, or two, or even one only, without breaking the (rules of) studentship, shall enter the order of householders.

3. He who is famous for (the strict performance of) his duties and has received his heritage, the Veda, from his father, shall be honoured, sitting on a couch and adorned with a garland, with (the present of) a cow (and the honey-mixture).

4. Having bathed, with the permission of his teacher, and performing according to the rule the Samāvartana (the rite on returning home), a twice-born man shall marry a wife of equal caste who is endowed with auspicious (bodily) marks.

75. Let (every man) in this (second order, at least) daily apply himself to the private recitation of the Veda, and also to the performance of the offering to the gods; for he who is diligent in the performance of sacrifices, supports both the movable and the immovable creation.

76. An oblation duly thrown into the fire, reaches the sun; from the sun comes rain, from rain (comes) food, therefrom the living creatures (derive their subsistence).
77. As all living creatures subsist by receiving support from air, even so (the members of) all orders subsist by receiving support from the householder.
78. Because men of the three (other) orders are daily supported by the householder with (gifts of) sacred knowledge and food, therefore (the order of) householders is the most excellent order.
79. (The duties of) this order, which cannot be practised by men with weak organs, must be carefully observed by him who desires imperishable (bliss in) heaven, and constant happiness in this (life).
80. The sages, the manes, the gods, the Bhūtas, and guests ask the householders (for offerings and gifts); hence he who knows (the law), must give to them (what is due to each).
81. Let him worship, according to the rule, the sages by the private recitation of the Veda, the gods by burnt oblations, the manes by funeral offerings (Śrāddha), men by (gifts of) food, and the Bhūtas by the Bali-offering. — *Manusmṛti* III.1-4; 75-81; tr. G. Bühler[2]

III

Then follow the rules for the third stage of life — that of the hermit. The last three verses are significant inasmuch as these allow for self-willed death on part of a hermit:

1. A twice-born Snātaka, who has thus lived according to the law in the order of householders, may, after taking a firm resolution and keeping his organs in

2. G. Bühler, tr., op. cit., pp. 74-75; 88-90.

subjection, dwell in the forest, duly (observing the rules given below):

2. When a householder sees his (skin) wrinkled, and (his hair) white, and the sons of his sons, then he may resort to the forest.

3. Abandoning all food raised by cultivation, and all his belongings, he may depart into the forest, either committing his wife to his sons, or accompanied by her.

4. Taking with him the sacred fire and the implements required for domestic (sacrifices), he may go forth from the village into the forest and reside there, duly controlling his senses.

5. Let him offer those five great sacrifices according to the rule, with various kinds of pure food fit for ascetics, or with herbs, roots, and fruit.

6. Let him wear a skin or tattered garment; let him bathe in the evening or in the morning; and let him always wear (his hair in) braids, the hair on his body, his beard, and his nails (being unclipped).

7. Let him perform the Bali-offering with such food as he eats, and give alms according to his ability; let him honour those who come to his hermitage with alms consisting of water, roots, and fruit.

8. Let him always be industrious in privately reciting the Veda; let him be patient of hardships, friendly (towards all), of collected mind, ever liberal and never a receiver of gifts, and compassionate towards all living creatures.

9. Let him offer, according to the law, the Agnihotra with three sacred fires, never omitting the new-moon and full-moon sacrifices at the proper time.

16. Let him not eat anything (grown on) ploughed (land), though it may have been thrown away by somebody,

nor roots and fruit grown in a village, though (he may be) tormented (by hunger).

17. He may eat either what has been cooked with fire, or what has been ripened by time; he either may use a stone for grinding, or his teeth may be his mortar.

18. He may either at once (after his daily meal) cleanse (his vessel for collecting food), or lay up a store sufficient for a month, or gather what suffices for six months or for a year.

19. Having collected food according to his ability, he may either eat at night (only), or in the day-time (only), or at every fourth meal-time, or at every eighth.

25. Having reposited the three sacred fires in himself, according to the prescribed rule, let him live without a fire, without a house, wholly silent, subsisting on roots and fruit,

26. Making no effort (to procure) things that give pleasure, chaste, sleeping on the bare ground, not caring for any shelter, dwelling at the root of trees.

27. From Brāhmaṇas (who live as) ascetics, let him receive alms, (barely sufficient) to support life, or from other householders of the twice-born (castes) who reside in the forest).

28. Or (the hermit) who dwells in the forest may bring (food) from a village, receiving it either in a hollow dish (of leaves), in (his naked) hand, or in a broken earthen dish, and may eat eight mouthfuls.

29. These and other observances must a Brāhmaṇa, who dwells in the forest diligently practise, and in order to attain complete (union with) the (supreme) Soul, (he must study) the various sacred texts contained in the Upaniṣads,

30. (As well as those rites and texts) which have been practised and studied by the sages (*Ṛṣis*), and by Brāhmaṇa householders, in order to increase their knowledge (of Brahman), and their austerity, and in order to sanctify their bodies;

31. Or let him walk, fully determined and going straight on, in a north-easterly direction, subsisting on water and air, until his body sinks to rest.

32. A Brāhmaṇa, having got rid of his body by one of those modes practised by the great sages, is exalted in the world of Brahman, free from sorrow and fear.

— *Manusmṛti* VI.1-9; 16-19; 25-32; tr. G Bühler[3]

IV

The last stage of his life in that of an ascetic or a renunciant.

33. But having thus passed the third part of (a man's natural term of) life in the forest, he may live as an ascetic during the fourth part of his existence, after abandoning all attachment to the worldly objects.

34. He who after passing from order to order, after offering sacrifices and subduing his senses, becomes, tired (with) giving alms and offerings of food, an ascetic, gains bliss after death.

35. When he has paid the three debts, let him apply his mind to (the attainment of) final liberation; he who seeks it without having paid (his debts) sinks downwards.

36. Having studied the Vedas in accordance with the rule, having begot sons according to the sacred law, and having offered sacrifices according to his ability, he

3. G. Bühler, tr., op. cit., pp. 198-204.

may direct his mind to (the attainment of) final liberation.

37. A twice-born man who seeks final liberation, without having studied the Vedas, without having begotten sons, and without having offered sacrifices, sinks downwards.

38. Having performed the Iṣṭi, sacred to the Lord of creatures (Prajāpati), where (he gives) all his property as the sacrificial fee, having reposited the sacred fires in himself, a Brāhmaṇa my depart from his house (as an ascetic).

39. Worlds, radiant in brilliancy, become (the portion) of him who recites (the texts regarding) Brahman and departs from his house (as an ascetic), after giving a promise of safety to all created beings.

40. For the twice-born man, by whom not the smallest danger even is caused to created beings, there will be no danger from any (quarter), after he is freed from his body.

41. Departing from his house fully provided with the means of purification (Pavitra), let him wander about absolutely silent, and caring nothing for enjoyments that may be offered (to him).

42. Let him always wander alone, without any companion, in order to attain (final liberation), fully understanding that the solidarity (man, who) neither forsakes nor is forsaken, gains his end.

43. He shall neither possess a fire, nor a dwelling, he may go to a village for his food, (he shall be) indifferent to everything, firm of purpose, meditating (and) concentrating his mind on Brahman.

44. A potsherd (instead of an alms-bowl), the roots of trees (for a dwelling), coarse worn-out garments, life in solitude and indifference towards everything, are the marks of one who has attained liberation.

45. Let him not desire to die, let him not desire to live; let him wait for (his appointed) time, as a servant (waits) for the payment of his wages.

46. Let him put down his foot purified by his sight, let him drink water purified by (straining with) a cloth, let him utter speech purified by truth, let him keep his heart pure.

47. Let him patiently bear hard words, let him not insult anybody, and let him not become anybody's enemy for the sake of his (perishable) body.

48. Against an angry man let him not in return show anger, let him bless when he is cursed, and let him not utter speech, devoid of truth, scattered at the seven gates.

49. Delighting in what refers to the Soul, sitting (in the postures prescribed by the Yoga), independent (of external help), entirely abstaining from sensual enjoyments, with himself for his only companion, he shall live in this world, desiring the bliss (of final liberation).

— *Manusmṛti* VI.33-49; tr. G. Bühler[4]

4. G. Bühler, tr., op. cit., pp. 204-07.

20

Puruṣārtha

I

Hindu axiology recognises four goals of human endeavour, with spiritual liberation (*mokṣa*) constituting a class by itself. The other three are: righteousness or spiritual merit (*dharma*), the acquisition of wealth or power (*artha*), and the gratification of desires (*kāma*). The four terms: *dharma, artha, kāma* and *mokṣa* can be variously translated. As to the issue of priority among the three (*mokṣa* apart), the matter is settled as follows in *Manusmṛti* II.224, given below in two translations:

> (Some declare that) the chief good consists in (the acquisition of) spiritual merit and wealth, (others place it) in (the gratification of desire and (the acquisition of) wealth (others) in (the acquisition of) spiritual merit alone, and (others say that the acquisition of) wealth alone is the chief good here; but the (correct) decision is that it consists of the aggregate of these three. — Tr. G. Bühler[1]

> Some say that *dharma* [virtue] and material gain are good, others that pleasure and material gain are good, and others that *dharma* alone or pleasure alone are good, but the correct position is that the three should coexist without harming each other. — tr. V. Raghavan[2]

---

1. G. Bühler, tr. *The Laws of Manu*, Delhi: Motilal Banarsidass, 2001 [1886], pp. 70-71.
2. See Wm. Theodore de Bary et al., eds., *Sources of Indian Tradition* (second edn., New York, Columbia University Press, 1958), p. 213.

II

Dharma or righteousness, both sacred and secular, was in general accorded the highest value.

> When there are all three, virtue, material gain and pleasure, their mutual superiority is in the order of their precedence.
>
> — *Kāmasūtra* I.2.14; tr. V. Raghavan[3]

III

Some Hindu thinkers glorified *artha* as the *puruṣārtha* above all others, both seriously and cynically. Kauṭilya states so seriously and Bhartṛhari somewhat cynically.

> "Of the three ends of human life, material gain is, verily, the most important." So says Kauṭilya. "On material gain depends the realisation of *dharma* and pleasure."
>
> — *Arthaśāstra*.1.7; tr. R.N. Dandekar[4]

> A man of wealth is held to be high-born,
> Wise, scholarly, and discerning;
> Eloquent and even handsome –
> All virtues are accessories to gold!
>
> — Bhartṛhari, *Nītīśataka*; tr. Barbara Stoler Miller[5]

IV

Some Hindu thinkers accord primacy to *kāma*, whether in terms of devotional philosophy or when hinting at even the divine inevitability of conjugality.

> Tossing about restlessly with mind melted, singing again and again and shedding tears, calling you forth as Narasiṁha [an incarnation of Viṣṇu] and seeking you everywhere, this beautiful girl is languishing.
>
> — *Tiruvāymooḷi* 2.4.1[6]

---

3. Wm. Theodore de Bary et al., p. 214.
4. Ibid.
5. Barbara Stoler Miller, tr., *Bhartrihari's Poems*, New York: Columbia University Press, 1967, p. 41.
6. Wm Theodore de Bary et al., eds., op. cit., p. 355.

We bow to the god whose sign is a sea serpent,
To Kāma, who makes the gods Śiva, Brahmā, and Viṣṇu
Slaves in dark chambers of doe-eyed women;
To Kāma, whose marvellous artifice eludes all words.
— Bhartṛhari, *Śṛṅgāraśataka*; tr. Barbara Stoler Miller.[7]

7. Barbara Stoler Miller, tr., op. cit., p. 107.

21

Veda

Introduction

The Vedas, collectively called Veda, are the oldest source of Hindu thought. They represent a body of literature which assumed its present shape over a period of almost a thousand years. The chronology of the Vedas is disputed. They may be provisionally assigned to a period extending from c. 1500 to 400 BCE.

These Vedas are the foundational scriptures of Hinduism. They are represented by a collection of four compilations, and each of the compilation, in turn, may be described as consisting of four strata.

These compilations (Saṁhitā) are known as the *Ṛg-Veda*, the *Yajur-Veda*, the *Sāma-Veda* and the *Atharva-Veda*. Of these, the *Ṛg-Veda* is the largest, consisting of over a thousand hymns which average ten stanzas in length, addressed to various gods, among whom Indra and Agni are often assigned place of pride. The *Yajur-Veda*, which is basically in prose with occasional metrical passages, is about two-third the size of the *Ṛg-Veda* and relies heavily on it. It adapts the hymns of ritual employment. The *Sāma-Veda*, which, half in size compared to the *Ṛg-Veda*, is in verse and adapts the hymns for philharmonic purposes. All but 99 of its over 1,500 verses are not drawn from the *Ṛg-Veda*.

As distinguished from the first three Vedas, the *Atharva-Veda*, which is in both prose and verse and half the size of the *Ṛg-Veda*, draws only a fifth of its material from the *Ṛg-Veda* and is believed to represent a compilation of popular beliefs and practices, as distinguished from the more hieratic nature of the other three. Its assimilation as the fourth Veda seems to have occurred over a period of time.

Of relatively greater significance than its division into the four Vedas, is the division of each of the four Vedas into four layers, each of which represents a successive stage in the growth of Vedic literature and contains doctrines and practices distinct to itself, though not unrelated to the rest of the Veda in general.

The Saṁhitā or Mantra portions are devotional in nature. The Brāhmaṇas, the next major division, are in prose and ritualistic in content. The Āraṇyakas, the third substratum, a subdivision of the Brāhmaṇas, represent texts which contain rituals to be pursued in the relative isolation of the hermitages; while the Upaniṣads, which appear as chapters of the Āraṇyakas, constitute the fourth layer. A period of two hundred to three hundred years is notionally assigned to each layer as representing a phase in the development of the Hinduism.

The above account, historical-critical in nature as developed by modern scholarship, may be supplemented in three ways by taking the more traditional material into account, to apprise oneself of the Hindu self-understanding of these texts:

(1) "According to the *Viṣṇu Purāṇa*, the original Veda, first revealed by God to the *ṛṣis*, consisted of one hundred thousand verses, and had four divisions. With the efflux of time these divisions got mixed up and many portions of the Vedas fell into obscurity. So, in the end of the Dvāpara age, Kṛṣṇa Dvaipāyana resuscitated the Vedic study and classified the work according to the four ancient divisions of *Ṛk*, *Yajus*, *Sāman*, and *Atharvan*. In order to perpetuate the study of the Vedas

in a proper form, he taught them to his four principal disciples. He gave the *Ṛg-Veda* to Paila, *Yajur-Veda* to Vaiśampāyana, *Sāmaveda* to Jaimini, and *Atharva-Veda* to Sumanta. As he reclassified the Vedas, he became renowned by the name of Veda-Vyāsa, i.e. classifier of the Vedas. This tradition is so strong among the Hindu scholars that it cannot but be accepted as having some historical basis."[1]

(2) According to the Hindu tradition the "content of the Veda may also be reclassified into (a) *karma-kāṇḍa* or ritual section, (b) *upāsanā-kāṇḍa* or meditation section and (3) *jñāna-kāṇḍa* or knowledge section. The Mantras and the Brāhmaṇas constitute *karma-kāṇḍa*, the Āraṇyakas, *upāsanā-kāṇḍa*, and the Upaniṣads, *jñāna-kāṇḍa*".[2]

(3) Musical recitation of the *Sāma* hymns was originally the special function of women.[3]

Selections from the Saṁhitā Portion
The logic underlying the selections

The most important single text of *ancient* Hinduism — Vedic as well as classical — on par in significance with the Lord's Prayer in Christianity, the *shahādah* in Islam and the Three Refuges in Buddhism, was the *Gāyatrī mantra*, once recited generally, but whose recitation gradually became restricted to the male members of the three higher castes; hence it is cited first.

---

1. Swami Sharvananda, "The Vedas and their Religious Teachings" in Haridas Bhattacharyya, ed., *The Cultural Heritage of India* , Calcutta: The Ramakrishna Mission Institute of Culture, 1958, vol. I, pp. 182-83, with some emendation.
2. T.M.P. Mahadevan, *Outlines of Hinduism*, p. 31.
3. A.S. Altekar, *The Position of Women in Hindu Civilization from Prehistorical Times to the Present Day*, Delhi: Motilal Banarsidass, 1973, p. 20; also see p. 197.

The most important single text of *modern* Hinduism, which is drawn directly from Vedic Hinduism, is the *Ṛg-Veda* I.164.46. Hence it is cited next.

The general significance of the Vedas in terms of later Hinduism has been summarised by T.M.P. Mahadevan as follows:

> Right from the known beginnings of Hindu religious thought there have been two chief currents — one which may be called the theistic and the other absolutistic. All forms of theism recognise a cosmic creator called God, whereas absolutism reduces the plurality of things to one non-dual spiritual reality. While many of the Vedic hymns are addressed to one form or the other of the Deity, there are some in which the metaphysical Absolute is celebrated. In the hymns of Indra and Varuṇa — the most prominent Vedic gods — we come nearest to monotheism. In what is known as the *Puruṣa-Sūkta* we have a view of God as immanent in the world as well as transcendent. In the *Nāsadīya* hymn which is an example of pure Vedic metaphysics, the nature of the Absolute is indicated as what lies beyond the reach of all categories. The seeds of theism and absolutism that are thus to be found in the Vedas germinate and grow to huge proportions in later Hinduism, and get embellished in great detail.[4]

If, to these remarks, we add the consideration that the various gods invoked in the *Ṛg-Veda*, according to one classification, belong to one of the three — the terrestrial, the atmospheric, and the celestial regions and that Agni, Indra, and Varuṇa are assigned to these respectively, we might wish to add hymns to Agni to our selection, especially as it was the god of the hearth, and the number of hymns dedicated to him are second in number only to Indra.[5] Nearly one-fourth of

4. T.M.P. Mahadevan, op. cit., p. 251.
5. V.M. Apte, "Religion and Philosophy", in R.C. Majumdar, ed., *The Vedic Age*, Bombay: Bharatiya Vidya Bhavan, 1965, p. 373.

the total hymns are addressed to Indra and Agni is "second in importance only to Indra".[6]

The selections, therefore, are placed in the following order:

1. The Gāyatrī,
2. *Ekam Sat,*
3. Hymns to Agni,
4. Hymns to Indra,
5. Hymns to Varuṇa,
6. Puruṣa-sūkta and
7. Nāsadīya Hymn.

Selections:

1. *Gāyatrī*

So called after the metre, its formal recitation constitutes initiation into Vedic studies.

> Let us think on the lovely splendour
> of the god Savitṛ,
> that he may inspire our minds.
> — III.62.10: tr. A.L. Basham[7]

Savitṛ is the solar deity or the sun in plain language, as the one who "stimulates". More details are offered below:

> Savitṛ is pre-eminently a golden deity. His eyes, arms, hands, and tongue are golden; so are his car and its pole. He diffuses golden splendour. He removes evil dreams and drives away demons and sorcerers. In the famous Gāyatrī stanza (III.62.10), which has remained the sacred morning prayer of the Hindus for more than two thousand years, he is invoked to confer his splendour on, and stimulate the thoughts of, the worshipper.[8]

6. Ibid., p. 376.
7. A.L. Basham, *The Wonder That was India*, New Delhi: Rupa & Co., 1999 [1967], p. 162.
8. V.M. Apte, op. cit., p. 367.

2. *Ekam Sat* (I.164.46)

The most often cited segment from the *Ṛg-Veda* in modern Hinduism as proof text of religious universalism, as well as the foundation of Hindu monism.

> The one reality is called by the wise in different ways: Agni, Yama, Mātriśvā.
>
> — *Ṛg-Veda* I.164.46b; tr. Chatterjee and Datta[9]

3. *Agni*

This is the first hymn of the Vedic corpus according to its traditional arrangement. The recitation of the *Ṛg-Veda* commences with this hymn to the god of Fire.

1. I magnify Agni, the *purohita*, the divine ministrant of the sacrifice, the Hotṛ priest, the greatest bestower of treasures.
2. Agni, worthy to be magnified by the ancient *ṛṣi*s and by the present ones — may he conduct the gods hither.
3. May one obtain through Agni wealth and welfare day by day, which may bring glory and high bliss of valiant offspring.
4. Agni, whatever sacrifice and worship thou encompassest on every side, that indeed goes to the gods.
5. May Agni the thoughtful Hotṛ, he who is true and most splendidly renowned, may the god come hither with the gods.
6. Whatever good thou wilt do to thy worshipper, O Agni, that (work) verily is thine, O Aṅgiras.
7. Thee, O Agni, we approach day by day, O (god) who is the shiniest in the darkness; with our prayer, bringing adoration to thee —

9. Satischandra Chatterjee and Dhirendramohan Datta, *An Introduction to Indian Philosophy*, New Delhi: Rupa & Co., 2007, p. 321.

8. Who art the king of all worship, the guardian of *ṛta*, the shining one, increasing in thy own house.
9. Thus, O Agni, be easy of access to us, as a father is to his son. Stay with us for our happiness.

— *Ṛg-Veda* I.1: tr. Hermann Oldenberg[10]

4. *Indra*

Indra, now a minor god in Hinduism, was the major god in the *Ṛg-Veda* and judged by the number of hymns dedicated to him, perhaps *the* major god in the pantheon. He is a god of the atmospheric region and hence appears often in association with thunder, wielding lightning as his weapon called *vajra* (thunderbolt). The most significant myth connected with him is the slaying of the demon Vṛtra, who was withholding the waters and the sun. The killing of Vṛtra released the waters to flow and the sun to shine. His dual role — as a martial god wielding the *vajra* and as a god facilitating rain — may reflect the two main concerns of the Aryan people: namely, the need to overcome adversaries and the need for water as essential for physical and economic survival. A hymn about him follows:

> Indra's heroic deeds, indeed, will I proclaim, the first ones which the wielder of the *vajra* accomplished. He killed the dragon, released the waters, and split open the sides of the mountains.
>
> He killed the dragon lying spread out on the mountain; for him Tvashtar fashioned the roaring vajra. Like bellowing cows, the waters, gliding, have gone down straightaway to the ocean.
>
> Showing off his virile power he chose *soma*; from the three *kadruka*s he drank of the extracted *soma*. The bounteous god took up the missile, the *vajra*; he killed the first-born among the dragons.

---

10. Hermann Oldenberg, *Vedic Hymns*, Oxford: Clarendon Press, 1897, Part II, p. 1.

When you, O Indra, killed the first-born among the dragons and further overpowered the wily tricks (*māyā*) of the tricksters, bringing forth, at that very moment, the sun, the heaven, and the dawn — since then, indeed, have you not come across another enemy.

Indra killed Vṛtra, the greater enemy, the shoulderless one, with his mighty and fatal weapon, the *vajra*. Like branches of a tree lopped off with an axe, the dragon lies prostrate upon the earth.

For, like an incapable fighter, in an intoxicated state, he [Vṛtra] had challenged the great hero [Indra], the mighty overwhelmer, the drinker of *soma*, to the dregs. He did not surmount the onslaught of his fatal weapon. Indra's enemy, broken [-nosed], was completely crushed.

Footless and handless he gave battle to Indra. He [Indra] struck him with the *vajra* upon the back. The castrated bull, seeking to become a compeer of the virile bull, Vṛtra lay shattered in many places.

Over him, who lay in that manner like a shattered reed, flowed the waters for the sake of man. At the feet of the very waters, which Vṛtra had [once] enclosed with his might, the dragon [now] lay [prostrate].

Vṛtra's mother had her vital energy ebbing out: Indra had hurled his fatal weapon at her. The mother lay above, the son below; Dānu lay down like a cow with her calf.

In the midst of the water-streams, which never stood still nor had any resting place, the body lay. The waters flow in all directions over Vṛtra's secret place; Indra's enemy lay sunk in long darkness.

With the Dāsa as their lord and with the dragon as their warder, the waters remained imprisoned, like cows held by Pani. Having killed Vṛtra, [Indra] threw open the cleft of waters which had been closed.

> You became the hair of a horse's tail, O Indra, when he [Vṛtra] struck at your sharp-pointed *vajra* — the one god (*eka deva*) though you were. You won the cows, O brave one, you won *soma*; you released the seven rivers, so that they should flow.
>
> Neither did lightning nor thunder, nor mist nor hailstorm, which he [Vṛtra] had spread out, prove efficacious when Indra and the dragon fought. And the bounteous god remained victorious for all time to come.
>
> Whom did you see, O Indra, as the avenger of the dragon, that fear entered into your heart, after you had killed the dragon, and frightened, you crossed nine and ninety rivers and the aerial regions like the falcon?
>
> Indra, who wields the *vajra* in his hand, is the lord of what moves and what remains rested, of what is peaceful and what is horned. He alone rules over the tribes as their king; he encloses them as does a rim the spokes. — *Ṛg-Veda* I.32, tr. R.N. Dandekar[11]

5. *Varuṇa*

M. Hiriyanna Explains:

> Indra, however, was not the sole type of divinity known to the Vedic Aryans, for there are clear, though not so frequent, references in these hymns to another important deity, Varuṇa, who is essentially a god of righteousness and is the guardian of all that is worthy and good. He is omniscient, and is described as ever witnessing the truth and falsehood of men — as being "the third whenever two plot in secret". He is not only able to find out the inmost sin of man, but is also beneficent and will graciously forgive the sinner, if he be truly penitent. "Set us free from the sin we have committed" is, indeed, the burden of every hymn

11. Wm. Theodore de Bary et al., eds., op. cit., pp. 13-15. Some words additionally italicized.

addressed to Varuṇa. The songs composed in his praise are some of the sublimest in the Veda.[12]

The Deeds of Varuṇa

The hymn describes the great deeds of Varuṇa and closes with a wish that he will pardon the mistakes of the worshipper.

> Unto the sovereign lord sing a sublime and solemn prayer (*brahman*), one dear unto glorious Varuṇa, who has spread out the earth, as the butcher does the hide, by way of a carpet for the sun.
>
> Varuṇa has extended the air above the trees; he has put strength in horses, milk in cows, will-power in hearts, fire in waters, the sun in the heaven, and soma upon the mountain.
>
> Varuṇa poured out the leather-bag, opening downward, upon the heaven and the earth and the mid-region. Thereby does the lord of the whole creation moisten thoroughly the expanse of earth, as rain does the corn.
>
> He moistens the broad earth and the heaven. When Varuṇa would have it milked [i.e., would shower rain] then, indeed, do the mountains clothe themselves with clouds and the heroes, showing off their might, loosen those clothes [i.e., disperse the clouds].
>
> This great magic-work (*māyā*) of the renowned spiritual Varuṇa will I proclaim loudly; of Varuṇa, who, standing in the mid-region, has measured the earth with the sun as with a measuring rod.
>
> No one, indeed, dare impugn this great magic-work of the wisest god, namely that the many glistening streams, pouring forth, do not fill up one ocean with water.
>
> If we, O Varuṇa, have offended against a friend,

12. M. Hiriyanna, op. cit., p. 12.

befriended through Aryaman or through Mitra [i.e., the gods of hospitality and friendship], or if we have offended against an all-time comrade or a brother or an inmate — whether belonging to us, O Varuṇa, or a stranger — do you remove that offence from us.

If we have deceived, like gamblers in a game of dice, and whether we really know it or not, all that do you unbind from us, like loosened fetters, O god. Thus may we be dear unto you, O Varuṇa.

— *Ṛg-Veda* V.85, tr. R.N. Dandekar[13]

6. *Puruṣa-sūkta*

This is the celebrated hymn to Man or the primeval person, theistic in bent.

The Puruṣa-sūkta (Hymn of Man)

A thousand heads hath Puruṣa, a thousand eyes, a thousand feet
On every side pervading earth he fills a space ten fingers wide.
This Puruṣa is all that yet hath been and all that is to be,
The lord of immortality which waxes greater still by food.
So mighty is his greatness; yea, greater than this is Puruṣa.
All creatures are one-fourth of him, three-fourths eternal life in heaven.
With three-fourths Puruṣa went up; one-fourth of him again was here.
Thence he strode out to every side over what eats not and what eats.
From him Virāj was born; again Puruṣa from Virāj was born.
As soon as he was born he spread eastward and

13. Wm. Theodore de Bary et. al., eds., op. cit., pp. 11-12.

westward o'er the earth.
When gods prepared the sacrifice with Puruṣa as their offering,
Its oil was spring; the holy gift was autumn; summer was the wood.
They balmed as victim on the grass Puruṣa born in the earliest time.
With him the deities and all Sādhyas and R̥ṣis sacrificed.
From that great general sacrifice the dripping fat was gathering up.
He formed the creatures of the air, and animals both wild and tame.
From that great general sacrifice r̥ks and Sāma-hymns were born;
Therefore were spells and charms produced; the Yajus had their birth from it.
From it were horses born, from it all cattle with two rows of teeth;
From it were gathered kine, from it the goats and sheep were born.

When they divided Puruṣa, how many portions did they make?

What do they call his mouth, his arms? What do they call
his thighs and feet?
The brāhmaṇa was his mouth, of both his arms was the Rājanya made.
His thighs became the vaiśya, from his feet the śūdra was produced.
The moon was gendered from his mind, and from his eye the sun had birth;
Indra and Agni from his mouth were born, and Vāyu from his breath.
Forth from his navel came the mid-air; the sky was fashioned from his head;
Earth from his feet, and from his ear the regions. Thus

they formed the worlds.
Seven fencing-sticks had he, thrice seven layers of fuel were prepared,
When the gods, offering sacrifice, bound, as their victim, *puruṣa*.
Gods, sacrificing, sacrificed the victim: these were the earliest holy ordinance.
The mighty ones attained the height of heaven, there where the *sādhyas*, gods of old, are dwelling.

— *R̥g-Veda* X.90, tr. Louis Renou[14]

7. *Nāsadīya Hymn*

1. Non-being then existed not, nor being:
There was no air, nor sky that is beyond it.
What was concealed? Wherein? In whose protection?
And was there deep unfathomable water?

2. Death then existed not, nor life immortal;
Of neither night nor day was any token.
By its inherent force the One breathed windless:
No other thing than that beyond existed.

3. Darkness there was at first by darkness hidden;
Without distinctive marks, this was all water.
That which, becoming, by the void was covered,
That One by force of heat came into being.

4. Desire entered the One in the beginning:
It was the earliest seed, of thought the product.
The sages searching in their hearts with wisdom,
Found out the bond of being in non-being.

5. Their ray extended light across the darkness:
But was the one above or was it under?
Creative force was there, and fertile power:
Below was energy, above was impulse.

6. Who knows for certain? Who shall here declare it?
Whence was it born, and whence came this creation?

---

14. Louis Renou, ed., op. cit., pp. 64-65.

The gods were born after this world's creation:
Then who can know from whence it has arisen?

7. None knoweth whence creation has arisen;
And whether he has or has not produced it:
He who surveys it in the highest heaven,
He only knows, or haply he may know not.

— *R̥g-Veda* X.129: tr. A.A. Macdonell[15]

Concluding Remarks

We end the selections on a note sounded this time by R.N. Dandekar, (with which he introduces the Nāsadīya hymn), which echoes the earlier remarks of T.M.P. Mahadevan.

> In the early Indra creation myth, the demon Vr̥tra had to be slain before creation could proceed. Indra as the personal demiurge brought order out of chaos (asat); that is to say, he brought about the existent (sat) from the non-existent (asat). In later Vedic cosmogenic speculation, the personal creator, Indra as the One God (*eka deva*) is conceived of as an impersonal creative impulse called That One (*tad ekam*). When the question arises as to "what enclosed all," the answer is no longer Vr̥tra according to the old myth, but rather that creation proceeds from a principle motivated by desire outside, or over and beyond, "being" and "non-being". In terms of this new cosmological interpretation of creation, only the sages were able to fathom in their hearts the relation of "being" and "non-being". The hymn ends on a note of scepticism, which anticipates the questioning mood of the Upaniṣads — "he who is the highest overseer in heaven, he certainly knows, on the other hand, perhaps he does not".[16]

---

15. As cited in Sarvepalli Radhakrishnan and Charles A. Moore, eds., *A Source Book of Indian Philosophy*, Princeton, New Jersey: Princeton University Press, 1957, pp. 23-24.
16. Wm. Theodore de Bary et al., eds., op. cit., p. 17.

Selections from the Brāhmaṇa Portion

Introduction

The Brāhmaṇas are among the earliest prose-texts of Hinduism. By this time the simple ritual which accompanied the early devotional hymns had become so elaborate that classes of professional priests had evolved to take care of them. Thus the Hotā, Udagātṛ, Adhvaryu, and Brāhmaṇa became specialists respectively of the *Ṛg-*, the *Sāma-*, the *Yajur-* and the *Atharva-Veda*.[17]

The use of the word Brāhmaṇa must be clarified before it causes any further confusion. This polyeomic word "means 'relating to Brahman or simply 'brahmanic'. Since the Veda contains both terms *bráhman* 'prayer' and *brahmán* 'pray-er', the Brāhmaṇas could be considered as either referring to the knowledge of *brahman* or as belonging to the priesthood . . . the former interpretation seems more likely."[18] The word thus possesses several meanings: (1) a spiritual one, meaning a knower of *Brahman* or the ultimate reality; (2) a social one, as meaning a member of the priestly class; (3) a textual one, as signifying "an authoritative utterance of a priest, relating particularly to sacrifice, and the Brāhmaṇas [as textual category] are so called because they are the repositories of such utterances",[19] and (4) a member of a priestly order connected with the *Atharva-Veda*.

One of the gods mentioned in the Vedas, namely Prajāpati, gains importance in the Brāhmaṇas, only to lose to this position at a later stage in the development of the Vedic religion.

The Logic Underlying the Selections

The first selection connects these two emerging salients of the

17. R.C. Majumdar, ed., *The Vedic Age*, p. 446.
18. Wm. Theodore de Bary et al., eds., op. cit., p. 20.
19. M. Hiriyanna, op. cit., p. 14.

Vedic religion in the Brāhmaṇa period — special status attained by priests, and the special status achieved by Prajāpati. The next selection is very different in character, indicative of the fact that the Brāhmaṇas are repositories not just of rituals but also of myths. The third selection reveals the high level of astronomical knowledge attained during the period. The last selection speaks for itself.

Selections

I. *Śatapatha Brāhmaṇa*

It is worth noting that just as in the Saṁhitās, so also in the Brāhmaṇas, the One — in this case Prajāpati, is called variously.

> The same (divine person), the Adhvaryus (*Yajur-Veda* priest) serve under the name of 'Agni' (fire-altar) and 'Yajus,' because he holds together (*yuj*) all this (universe); the Chandogas (*Sāma-veda* priests, chanters) under that of 'Sāman,' because in him all this (universe) is one and the same (*samāna*); the *Bahvrika*s (*Ṛg-Veda* priests, *Hotar*s) under that of *Uktham* because he originates (*utthāp*) everything here; those skilled in sorcery, under that of 'sorcery' (*yātu*), because everything here is held in check (*yata*) by him; the serpents under that of 'poison'; the snake-charmers under that of 'snake'; the gods under that of *ūrg* (strengthening food); men under that of 'wealth'; demons under that of *māyā* (magic power); the deceased fathers under that of *svadhā* (invigorating draught); those knowing the divine host under that of 'divine host'; the *gandharva*s under that of form (*rūpa*); the *apsara*s under that of fragrance (*gandha*), — thus, in whatsoever form they serve him that indeed he becomes, and, having become that, he is helpful to them; whence he who knows should serve him in all

these (forms), for he becomes all that, and, having become all that, he is helpful to him.

— *Śatapatha Brāhmaṇa*, X.5.2.20; tr. Julius Eggeling[20]

In the morning they brought to Manu water for washing, just as now also they are wont to bring water for washing the hands. When he was washing himself, a fish came into his hands.

It spake to him the word, "Rear me, I will save thee!" "Wherefrom wilt thou save me?" "A flood will carry away all these creatures: from that I will save thee!" "How am I to rear thee?"

It said, "As long as we are small, there is great destruction for us: fish devours fish. Thou wilt keep me in a jar. When I outgrow that, thou wilt dig a pit and keep me in it. When I outgrow that, thou wilt take me down the sea, for then I shall be beyond destruction."

It soon became a large fish. Thereupon it said, "In such and such a year that flood will come. Thou shalt then attend to my advice by preparing a ship; and when the flood has risen thou shalt enter into the ship, and I will save thee from it."

After he had reared it in this way, he took it down to the sea. And in the same year which the fish had indicated to him, he attended to the advice of the fish by preparing a ship; and when the flood had risen, he entered into the ship. The fish then swam up to him, and to its horn he tied the rope of the ship, and by that means he passed swiftly up to yonder northern mountain.

It then said, "I have saved thee. Fasten the ship to a tree; but let not the water cut thee off, whilst thou art

---

20. Julius Eggeling, tr., *The Śatapatha-Brāhmaṇa According to the Text of Mādhyandina School* (Delhi: Motilal Banarsidass, 1963 [1897]), Part IV, pp. 373-74. Also see Herman Tull, *The Vedic Origins of Karma* (Delhi: Satguru Publications, 1990 [1989]), p. 58.

> on the mountain. As the water subsides, thou mayest gradually descend!" Accordingly he gradually descended, and hence that slope of the northern mountain is called "Manu's descent!" The flood then swept away all these creatures, and Manu alone remained here.
>
> — *Śatapatha Brāhmaṇa* I.8.1.1-6: tr. Louis Renou[21]

II. *Aitareya Brāhmaṇa*

The following passage demonstrates that the Vedic Hindus apparently knew by now that the sun is stationary in relation to the earth, contrary to the optical illusion of its rising and setting. The Brāhmaṇas are often accused of being excessively ritualistic, and the consequent aversion which a rational mind experiences has sometimes led it to neglect such observations.

> This *āditya* (the sun) never sets and never rises. When one thinks him to have set, actually he creates night in that part and day in the other part (of the globe) at that time. When in the morning one regards the sun to have risen, in reality he terminates the night and creates day in that part; the other part being enveloped in night at that time. This sun never sets.
>
> — *Aitareya Brāhmaṇa* III-14: tr. Jogiraj Basu[22]

III. *Taittirīya Brāhmaṇa Kāṭhaka*

Classical Hindu tradition is based on the Vedas and contains much praise of the Vedas. The Vedas as a concept, however, have not escaped that plurality of interpretations which characterises the tradition which traces itself back to it.[23] Here is one interpretation based on the Brāhmaṇas, with text and translation:

---

21. Louis Renou, ed., op. cit., pp. 84-85.
22. Jogiraj Basu, *India of the Age of the Brāhmaṇas,* Calcutta: Sanskrit Pustak Bhandar, 1969, p. 266.
23. See K. Satchidananda Murty, *Vedic Hermeneutics,* Delhi: Motilal Banarsidass, 1993.

Anantā vai Vedāḥ?
Vedas are many — *Taittirīya Brāhmaṇa Kāṭhaka* I.IX.4:
tr. T.M.P. Mahadevan[24]

In order to realise the full potential of this statement, one must read the following remarks by T.M.P. Mahadevan to the very end: "For a long time, in the history of Hinduism, it was considered a sacrilege to write a religious or philosophical work in any of the popular languages of India. But, if the truths of religion and philosophy are to be brought home to the mind of the commoner, Sanskrit which is a difficult tongue to learn, requiring considerable effort and application, will not be of much avail. Even from the earliest time we find the protest movements making use of the local dialects for purposes of propagating their views. The early Buddhist literature is in Pāli. The Jainas wrote their early books in Ardhamāgadhi. But these two schools soon realised that they would not gain philosophical recognition if their thoughts were not dressed in Sanskrit, with the result that the later works of these schools came to be written in that language. But with the march of time this attitude changed, and we have today a mass of philosophical and religious literature in each of the popular languages. To instance but a few, the *Tevāram* and the *Tiruvācakam* are well known among the hymns of the Śaiva saints of south India; the Vaiṣṇavas have correspondingly the *Divyaprapandham* and other devotional songs; the Caitanya movement and the songs of Tagore are responsible for the enrichment of Bengali devotional literature; the songs of Kabīr, the *Abhaṅgas* of the Maharashtra saints, the *Rāmāyaṇa* of Tulsīdās are all outpourings of god-intoxicated souls. If the essentials of Hinduism have found a place, difficult to dislodge, in the home of even the lowliest and the last in this vast country, it is not a little due to these devotional poems in the languages

24. T.M.P. Mahadevan, op. cit., p. 39.

of the people. To all of them the name 'Veda' may be given, for has not the Veda itself declared that the Vedas are many, unending (*anantā vai vedhā!*)"[25]

From the Āraṇyaka Portion

Introduction

The Āraṇyakas mark the transition from the Brāhmaṇas to the more popular Upaniṣads and sometimes get lost in the shuffle. They are often translated as forest-books but scholars noted long ago that these texts were really meant to deal with sacrifices, which were performed in the wilderness. Many passages prefigure the kind of reflection which became so characteristic of the Upaniṣads and this fact provides the logic underlying the selection of the following passage.

Selection

Who is he who we meditate on as the self? Which is that self? That by which one sees, by which one hears, by which one smells scents, by which one forms speech, by which one discriminates sweet and sour? That which is the heart and the mind, perception, injunction, understanding, knowledge, wisdom, vision, firmness, thinking, considering, helping, memory, resolution, will, breath, love, and desire? All these are only names of knowledge. That (self) is *brahman*, Indra, Prajāpati, all the gods, the five great elements, earth, ether, water, lights, all these and those which are mixed with small as it were, seeds of various kinds, born of eggs, born from the womb, born from heat, born from germs, horses, cows, men, elephants, and all that breathes, whether it walks or flies, and what is immovable. All that is guided by knowledge, it rests on knowledge. The world is guided by knowledge. Knowledge is its foundation. Knowledge is *brahman*. He by

25. T.M.P. Mahadevan, op. cit., pp. 38-39.

his knowing self having left this world and having obtained all delights in the world of heaven became immortal.

— *Aitareya Āraṇyaka* II.6: tr. A.B. Keith[26]

From the Upaniṣad Portion

Introduction

The Upaniṣads by now hardly require any introduction. They constitute both the coping stone of Vedic Hinduism and the cornerstone of Classical Hinduism. They have also already been cited extensively. Nevertheless, it would be worthwhile to look at some passages not explored earlier.

The Logic Underlying the Selections

The logic for the selection of these passages is traditional — it at least embodies one tradition. Classical Hinduism selected certain *mahāvākya*s (mighty utterances) of the Upaniṣads as quintessential. This selection is primarily prevalent in the non-dualistic tradition of interpreting the Upaniṣads, although the other philosophical schools have also offered their own explanations of these utterances.

It might be a good idea to examine the context of these utterances. A tetrad of such utterances is widely celebrated, although there is some difference on exactly which four are comprised by the tetrad. The two optional listings are as follows:

(1) *tat tvam asi*
That thou art — *Chāndogya Upaniṣad* VI.8.6

(2) *aham brahmāsmi*
I am *Brahman* — *Bṛhadāraṇyaka Upaniṣad* I.4.10

(3) *ayamātmā brahma*

26. Arthur Berriedale Keith, *The Aitareya Āraṇyaka*, Oxford: Clarendon Press, 1909, pp. 234-36.

This *ātman* is *Brahman*

— *Bṛhadāraṇyaka Upaniṣad* IV.4.5; *Māṇḍūkya Upaniṣad* 2

(4) *sarvam khalvidaṁ brahma*
All this verily is *Brahman.*

— *Chāndogya Upaniṣad* III.14.1

In the optional listing, the fourth is replaced by *prajñānam brahma,* or Knowledge is *Brahman* (*Aitareya Upaniṣad* V.3).[27]

It is even claimed that each of the *mahāvākyas* is associated with one of the four great centres Śaṅkara established in the four corners of India. Thus we learn that:

> Śaṅkara insisted on rigorous discipline and intellectual activity. He founded bulwarks of Advaita in the four corners of India. Vimalā Pīṭha at Jagannāth/Purī on the east coast, with which the Āraṇyas and Vānas are associated, who have as their mantra, "*prajñānam brahma*". Jyotiṛ Maṭha, near Badrināth in the Himālayas, is the centre of the Giri, Parvata, and Sāgara, with the mantra, "*ayam ātman brahma*". Kālikā Pīṭha in Dvārkā on the West Coast, with the Tīrthas and Āśramas, having as their mantra: "*tat tvam asi.*" Śāradā Maṭha in Dvārakā on the west coast is home to the *Tīrthas* and *Āśramas*, who have as their mantra, "*tat tvam asi*". Śṛṅgerī Maṭha in south India is the base of the Bhāratis, Pūrīs, and Sarasvatīs, with the mantra, "*aham brahmāsmi*". The *ācārya* of the last one is considered to be the actual head of the entire order, addressed as *jagadguru*, spiritual master of the whole world.[28]

27. K. Satchidananda Murty, *Revelation and Reason in Advaita Vedānta,* Waltair: Andhra University and New York: Columbia University, 1959, pp. 74-75.

28. Klaus K. Klostermaier, *A Survey of Hinduism* (2nd edn.), p. 350, with slight modifications.

The terms such as Āraṇya, Tīrtha, Bhāratī, etc. refer to the vaious name-endings adopted by the monks of the Dāśanāmī Order upon initiation.

Selections

Out of these four/five *mahāvākyas*,"That Thou Art" is perhaps the most celebrated. We therefore favour its selection. The manner of instruction deserves special notice. The manner of instruction in modern education is impersonal and conceptual. The mode of instruction in ancient India was personal and experiential. Such instruction was imparted by master to disciple or father to son. The following passage indicates both what was taught and how it was taught.

Sixth Prapāṭhaka

The instruction of Śvetaketu by Uddālaka concerning the key to all knowledge.

First Khaṇḍa

The threefold development of the elements and of man from the primary unitary Being:

1. *oṁ*! Now, there was Śvetaketu Āruṇeya. To him his father said: "Live the life of a student of sacred knowledge. Verily, my dear, from our family there is no one unlearned [in the Vedas] (*an-ucya*), a Brahman by connection (*brahmabandhu*), as it were."
2. He then, having become a pupil at the age of twelve, having studied all the Vedas, returned at the age of twenty-four, conceited, thinking himself learned, proud.
3. Then his father said to him: "Śvetaketu, my dear, since now you are conceited, think yourself learned, and are proud, did you also ask for that teaching whereby what has not been heard of becomes heard of, what has not been thought of becomes thought of, what has not been understood becomes understood?"

4. "How, pray, sir, is that teaching?"

   "Just as, my dear, by one piece of clay everything made of clay may be known — the modification is merely a verbal distinction, a name; the reality is just 'clay'", —

5. "Just as, my dear, by one copper ornament everything made of copper may be known — the modification is merely a verbal distinction, a name; the reality is just 'copper'" —

6. "Just as, my dear, by one nail-scissors everything made of iron may be known — the modification is merely a verbal distinction, a name; the reality is just 'iron' — so, my dear, is that teaching."

7. "Verily, those honoured men did not know this; for, if they had known it, why would they not have told me? But do you sir, tell me it."

   "So be it, my dear", said he.

Second Khaṇḍa

1. "In the beginning, my dear, this world was just Being (*sat*), one only, without a second. To be sure, some people say: 'In the beginning this world was just Non-being (*a-sat*), one only, without a second; from that Non-being Being, was produced.'"

2. "But verily, my dear, whence could this be?" said he. "How from Non-being could Being be produced? On the contrary, my dear, in the beginning this world was just Being, one only, without a second".

3. It bethought itself: "Would that I were many! Let me procreate myself!" It emitted heat. That heat bethought itself: "Would that I were many! Let me procreate myself." It emitted water. Therefore, whenever a person grieves or perspires from the heat, then water [i.e. either tears or perspiration] is produced.

4. That water bethought itself: "Would that I were many! Let me procreate myself." It emitted food. Therefore whenever it rains, then there is abundant food. So food for eating is produced just from water.

Third Khaṇḍa

1. Now, of these beings here there are just three origins: [there are beings] born from an egg, born from a living thing, born from a sprout.
2. That divinity [i.e. Being] bethought itself: "Come! Let me enter these three divinities [i.e. heat, water, and food] with this living Soul (*ātman*), and separate out name and form.
3. Let me make each one of them threefold." That divinity entered into these three divinities with this living Soul, and separated out name and form.
4. It made each of them threefold.

Now, verily, my dear, understand from me how each of these three divinities becomes threefold.

Fourth Khaṇḍa

1. Whatever red form fire has, is the form of heat; whatever white, the form of water; whatever dark, the form of food. The firehood has gone from fire: the modification is merely a verbal distinction, a name. The reality is just "the three forms".
2. Whatever red form the sun has, is the form of heat; whatever white, the form of water; whatever dark, the form of food. The sunhood has gone from the sun: the modification is merely a verbal distinction, a name. The reality is just "the three forms".
3. Whatever red form the moon has, is the form of heat; whatever white, the form of water; whatever dark,

the form of food. The moonhood has gone from the moon: the modification is merely a verbal distinction, a name. The reality is just "the three forms".

4. Whatever red form the lightning has, is the form of heat; whatever white, the form of water; whatever dark, the form of food. The lightninghood has gone from the lightning: the modification is merely a verbal distinction, a name. The reality is just "the three forms".
5. Verily, it was just this that the great householders, greatly learned in sacred lore, knew when they said of old: "No one now will bring up to us what has not been heard of, what has not been thought of, what has not been understood." For from these [three forms] they knew [everything].
6. They knew that whatever appeared red was the form of heat. They knew that whatever appeared white was the form of water. They knew that whatever appeared dark was the form of food.
7. They knew that whatever appeared un-understood is a combination of just these divinities.

Verily, my dear, understand from me how each of these three divinities, upon reaching man becomes threefold.

Fifth Khaṇḍa

1. "Food, when eaten, becomes divided into three parts. That which is its coarsest constituent becomes the faeces; that which is medium, the flesh; that which is finest, the mind.
2. Water, when drunk, becomes divided into three parts. That which is its coarsest constituent becomes the urine; that which is medium, the blood; that which is finest, the breath (*prāṇa*).

3. Heat, when eaten, becomes divided into three parts. That which is its coarsest constituent becomes bone; that which is medium, the marrow; that which is finest, the voice.
4. For, my dear, the mind consists of food; the breath consists of water; the voice consists of heat."

"Do you, sir, cause me to understand even more." "So be it, my dear", said he.

Sixth Khaṇḍa

1. "Of coagulated milk, my dear, when churned, that which is the finest essence all moves upward; it becomes butter.
2. Even so, verily, my dear, of food, when eaten, that which is the finest essence all moves upward; it becomes the mind.
3. Of water, my dear, when drunk, that which is the finest essence all moves upward; it becomes the breath.
4. Of heat, my dear, when eaten, that which is the finest essence all moves upward; it becomes the voice.
5. For, my dear, the mind consists of food; the breath consists of water; the voice consists of heat."

"Do you, sir, cause me to understand even more." "So be it, my dear", said he.

Seventh Khaṇḍa

1. "A person, my dear, consists of sixteen parts. For fifteen days do not eat; drink water at will. Breath, which consists of water, will not be cut off from one who drinks water."
2. Then for fifteen days he did not eat. So then he approached him, saying, "What shall I say, sir?"

"The Ṛg verses, my dear, the Yajus formulas, the Sāman chants."

Then he said: "Verily, they do not come to me, sir."

3. To him he then said: "Just us, my dear, a single coal of the size of a fire-fly may be left over from a great kindled fire, but with it the fire would not thereafter burn much — so, my dear, of your sixteen parts a single sixteenth part may be left over, but with it you do not now apprehend the Vedas. Eat; then you will understand from me."

4. Then he ate. So then he approached him. Then whatsoever he asked him, he answered everything.

5. To him he then said:

"Just as, my dear, one may, by covering it with straw, make a single coal of the size of a fire-fly that has been left over from a great kindled fire blaze up, and with it the fire would thereafter burn much —

6. So, my dear, of your sixteen parts a single sixteenth part has been left over. After having been covered with food, it has blazed up. With it now apprehend the Vedas; for, my dear, the mind consists of food, the breath consists of water, the voice consists of heat."

The he understood from him — yea, he understood.

Eighth Khaṇḍa

Concerning sleep, hunger and thirst, and dying:

1. Then Uddālaka Āruṇi said to Śvetaketu, his son: Understand from me, my dear, the condition of sleep. When a person here sleeps (*svapiti*), as it is called, then, my dear, he has reached Being, he has gone to his own (*svam apīta.*) Therefore they say of him "he sleeps"; for he has gone to his own.

2. As a bird fastened with a string, after flying in this direction and in that without finding an abode elsewhere, rests down just upon its fastening — even so, my dear, the mind, after flying in this direction and in that without finding an abode elsewhere, rests down just upon breath; for the mind, my dear, has breath as its fastening.

3. Understand from me, my dear, hunger (*aśanā*) and thirst. When a person here is hungry (*aśiśiṣati*), as it is called, just water is leading off (*nayanti*) that which has been eaten (√*aś*). So, as they speak of "a leader-of-cows" (*go-nāya*), "a leader-of-horses" (*aśva-nāya*), "a leader-of-men" (*puruṣa-nāya*), so they speak of water as "a leader-of-food" (*aśa-nāya*, hunger).

   On this point, my dear, understand that this [body] is a sprout which has sprung up. It will not be without a root.

4. What else could its roots be than food? Even so, my dear, with food for a sprout, look for water as the root. With water, my dear, as a sprout, look for heat as the root. With heat, my dear, as a sprout, look for Being as the root. All creatures here, my dear, have Being as their root, have Being as their home, have Being as their support.

5. Now, when a person here is thirsty, as it is called, just heat is leading off that which has been drunk. So, as they speak of "a leader-of-cows" (*go-nāya*), "a leader-of-horses" (*aśva-nāya*), "a leader-of-men" (*puruṣa-nāya*), so one speaks of heat as "a leader-of-water" (*uda-nyā*, thirst).

   On this point, my dear, understand that this [body] is a sprout which has sprung up. It will not be without a root.

6. Where else could its root be than in water? With water, my dear, as a sprout, look for heat as the root. With

heat, my dear, as a sprout, look for Being as the root. All creatures here, my dear, have Being as their root, have Being as their home, have Being as their support.

But how, verily, my dear, each of these three divinities, upon reaching man, becomes threefold, has previously been said.

When a person here is deceasing, my dear, his voice goes into his mind; his mind, into his breath; his breath, into heat; the heat, into the highest divinity.

7. That which is the finest essence — this whole world has that as its soul. That is Reality (*satya*). That is Ātman (soul). That art thou, Śvetaketu.'

'Do you, sir, cause me to understand even more.'

'So be it, my dear,' said he.

Ninth Khaṇḍa

The unitary World-Soul,
the immanent reality of all things and of man:

1. 'As the bees, my dear, prepare honey by collecting the essences of different trees and reducing the essence to a unity,
2. as they are not able to discriminate "I am the essence of this tree", "I am the essence of that tree" — even so, indeed, my dear, all creatures here, though they reach Being, know not "We have reached Being."
3. Whatever they are in this world, whether tiger, or lion, or wolf, or boar, or worm, or fly, or gnat, or mosquito, that they become.
4. That which is the finest essence — this whole world has that as its soul. That is Reality. That is Ātman (Soul). That art thou, Śvetaketu.'

'Do you, sir, cause me to understand even more.'

'So be it, my dear', said he.

Tenth Khaṇḍa

1. 'These rivers, my dear, flow, the eastern towards the east, the western towards the west. They go just from the ocean to the ocean. They become the ocean itself. As there they know not "I am this one", "I am that one" —
2. even so, indeed, my dear, all creatures here, though they have come forth from Being, know not "We have come forth from Being." Whatever they are in this world, whether tiger, or lion, or wolf, or boar, or worm, or fly, or gnat, or mosquito, that they become.
3. That which is the finest essence — this whole world has that as its soul. That is Reality. That is Ātman (Soul). That art thou, Śvetaketu.'

'Do you, sir, cause me to understand even more.'

'So be it, my dear,' said he.

Eleventh Khaṇḍa

1. 'Of this great tree, my dear, if some should strike at the root, it would bleed, but still live. If someone should strike at its middle, it would bleed, but still live. If some one should strike at its top, it would bleed, but still live. Being pervaded by Ātman (Soul), it continues to stand, eagerly drinking in moisture and rejoicing.
2. If the life leaves one branch of it, then it dries up. It leaves a second; then it dries up. It leaves a third; then that dries up. It leaves the whole; the whole dries up. Even so, indeed, my dear, understand', said he.
3. 'Verily, indeed, when life has left it, the body dies. The life does not die.

That which is the finest essence — this whole world has that as its soul. That is Reality. That is Ātman (Soul). That art thou, Śvetaketu.'

'Do you, sir, cause me to understand even more.'

'So be it, my dear,' said he.

Twelfth Khaṇḍa

1. 'Bring hither a fig from there.'
   'Here it is, sir.'
   'Divide it.'
   'It is divided, sir.'
   'What do you see there?'
   'There rather (*iva*) fine seeds, sir.'
   'Of these, please (*aṅga*), divide one.'
   'It is divided, sir.'
   'What do you see there?'
   'Nothing at all, sir.'
2. Then he said to him: 'Verily, my dear, that finest essence which you do not perceive — verily, my dear, from that finest essence this great Nyagrodha (sacred fig) tree thus arises.
3. Believe me, my dear', said he, 'that which is the finest essence — this whole world has that as its soul. That is Reality. That is Ātman (Soul). That art thou, Śvetaketu.'

'Do you, sir, cause me to understand even more.'

'So be it, my dear,' said he.

Thirteenth Khaṇḍa

1. 'Place this salt in the water. In the morning come unto me.'
   Then he did so.
   Then he said to him: 'that salt you placed in the water last evening — please bring it hither'.

Then he grasped for it, but did not find it, as it was completely dissolved.

2. 'Please take a sip of it from this end', said he. 'How is it?'

   'Salt.'
   'Take a sip from the middle', said he. 'How is it?'
   'Salt.'
   'Take a sip from that end', said he. 'How is it?'
   'Salt.'
   'Set it aside. Then come unto me.'
   He did so, saying, 'It is always the same.'

Then he said to him: 'Verily, indeed, my dear, you do not perceive Being here. Verily, indeed, it is here.

3. That which is the finest essence – this whole world has that as its soul. That is Reality. That is Ātman (Soul). That art thou, Śvetaketu.'

'Do you, sir, cause me to understand even more.'

'So be it, my dear,' said he.

Fourteenth Khaṇḍa

1. 'Just as, my dear, one might lead away from the Gandhāras a person with his eyes bandaged, and then abandon him in an uninhabited place; as there he might be blown forth either to the east, to the north, or to the south, since he has been led off with his eyes bandaged and deserted with his eyes bandaged;

2. as, if one released his bandage and told him, "In that direction are the Gandhāras; go in that direction!" he would, if he were a sensible man, by asking [his way] from village to village, and being informed, arrive home at the Gandhāras — even so here on earth one who has a teacher knows: "I shall remain here only so long as I shall not be released [from the bonds of ignorance]. Then I shall arrive at home."

3. That which is the finest essence — this whole world has that as its soul. That is Reality. That is Ātman (Soul). That art thou, Śvetaketu.'

'Do you, sir, cause me to understand even more.'

'So be it, my dear', said he.

Fifteenth Khaṇḍa

1. 'Also, my dear, around a [deathly] sick person his kinsmen gather, and ask, "Do you know me?" "Do you know me?" So long as his voice does not go into his mind, his mind into his breath, his breath into heat, the heat into the highest divinity — so long he knows.
2. Then when his voice goes into his mind, his mind into his breath, his breath into heat, that heat into the highest divinity — then he knows not.
3. That which is the finest essence — this whole world has that as its soul. That is Reality. That is Ātman (Soul). That art thou, Śvetaketu.'

'Do you, sir, cause me to understand even more.'

'So be it, my dear,' said he.

Sixteenth Khaṇḍa

1. 'And also, my dear, they lead up a man seized by the hand, and call: "He has stolen! He has committed a theft! Heat the axe for him!" If he is the doer thereof, thereupon he makes himself (*ātmānam*) untrue. Speaking untruth, covering himself with untruth, he seizes hold of the heated axe and is burned. Then he is slain.
2. But if he is not the doer thereof, thereupon he makes himself true. Speaking truth, covering himself with truth, he seizes hold of the heated axe and is not burned. Then he is released.

3. As in this case he would not be burned [because of the truth], so this whole world has that [truth] as its soul. That is Reality. That is Ātman (Soul). That art thou, Śvetaketu.'

Then he understood from him — yea, he understood.

— *Chāndogya Upaniṣad* VI.1-16: tr. R.E. Hume[29]

29. Robert Ernest Hume, tr., op. cit., pp. 240-50.

Concluding Remarks

It has been calculated that it would take a diligent student seventy lifetimes to read through the corpus of Hindu literature! Had the doctrine of rebirth not surfaced within Hinduism early enough, it is tempting to speculate that this fact alone might have given rise to it, in a brave mind not daunted by his prospect. Be that as it may, it should be clear that a selection of readings such as this requires no apology.

As I take the leave of the reader, I would like to refer to a few aspects of the present work which might enable him or her to utilise it better.

(1) This book is a sourcebook of Hindu thought rather than practice, and of classical Hindu thought at that. Hence it focuses on doctrine rather than practice, which might explain, for instance, the absence of certain kinds of material, such as deals with ritual or cultic practices, for example.

(2) Hindu classical thought is presented here in terms of its key concepts, thus involving a selection, as it were, before the selections themselves! The logic of this was explained in the Preface, as well as the order underlying the presentation of the concepts selected.

(3) Ironic as it may sound, in some cases it seemed that what outsiders had to say about classical Hinduism, or what some modern scholars have said about the classical themes, seemed so insightful that such material was also included, and the reader may have had to

practise the willing suspension of a sense of history for the duration. This may not be too excessive a demand in the study of a tradition which allegedly lacks a sense of it altogether!

(4) Although this book stands by itself, the reader may wish to read it as a companion volume of *Classical Hindu Thought*: *An Introduction*.

Finally, it might be not without interest to conclude these selections on classical Hindu thought, with an account of the encounter (or non-encounter, as we shall see) of Alexander with a classical Hindu thinker, Dandamis.

> King Alexander, accordingly, when he heard of all this, was desirous of learning the doctrine of the sect, and so he sent for this Dandamis, as being their teacher and president. . . .
>
> Onesicritus was therefore despatched to fetch him and when he found the great sage he said: "Hail to thee, thou teacher of the Bragmanes. The son of the mighty god Zeus, King Alexander, who is the sovereign lord of all men, asks you to go to him, and of you comply, he will reward you with great and splendid gifts, but if you refuse will cut off your head."
>
> Dandamis, with a complacent smile, heard him to the end, but did not so much as lift up his head from his couch of leaves, and while still retaining his recumbent attitude returned this scornful answer: "God, the Supreme King, is never the author of insolent wrong, but is the creator of light, of peace, of life, of water, of the body of man, and of souls. He alone is the god of my homage, who abhors slaughter and instigates no wars. But Alexander is not God, since he must taste of death; and how can such as he be the world's master, who has not yet reached the further shore of the river Tiberaboas, and has not yet seated himself on a throne

of universal dominion?. . . Know this, however, that what Alexander offers me, and the gifts he promises, are all things to me utterly useless; but the things I prize, and find of real use and worth, are these leaves which are my house, these blooming plants which supply me with dainty food, and the water which is my drink, while all other possessions and things, which are amassed with anxious care, are wont to prove ruinous to those who amass them, and cause only sorrow and vexation, with which every poor mortal is fully fraught. But as for me, I lie upon the forest leaves, and having nothing which requires guarding, close my eyes in tranquil slumber; whereas had I gold to guard, that would banish sleep. The earth supplies me with everything, even as a mother her child with milk. I go wherever I please, and there are no cares with which I am forced to cumber myself, against my will. Should Alexander cut off my head, he cannot also destroy my soul. My head alone, now silent, will remain, but the soul will go away to its Master, leaving the body like a torn garment upon the earth, whence also it was taken. I then, becoming spirit, shall ascend to my God, who enclosed us in flesh, and left us upon the earth to prove whether, when here below, we shall live obedient to his ordinances, and who also will require of us, when we depart hence to his presence, an account of our life, since he is judge of all proud wrong-doing; for the groans of the oppressed become the punishments of the oppressors.

"Let Alexander, then, terrify with these threats those who wish for gold and for wealth, and who dread death, for against us these weapons are both alike powerless, since the Bragmanes neither love gold nor fear death. Go, then, and tell Alexander this: 'Dandamis has no need of aught that is yours, and therefore will not go to you, but if you want anything from Dandamis come you to him.'"

Alexander, on receiving from Onesicritus a report of the interview, felt a stronger desire than ever to see Dandamis, who, though old and naked, was the only antagonist in whom he, the conqueror of many nations, had found more than his match.[1]

1. See R.C. Majumdar, ed., *The Age of Imperial Unity*, Bombay: Bharatiya Vidya Bhavan, 1951, pp. 554-55.

Notes on Sources Cited

***Śāṅkarabhāṣya* (or the commentary by Śaṅkara):** Śaṅkara (*c.* seventh/eighth century CE) wrote commentaries on all the Upaniṣads cited in these pages, as well as on the *Brahmasūtra* — an aphoristic distillation of the Upaniṣads, and on the *Bhagavad-Gītā*.

***Vivekacūḍāmaṇi* (Crest Jewel of Discrimination):** a general introduction to the Advaita Vedānta in verse, ascribed to Śaṅkara, and popular in the Advaitic circles.

***Saundaryalaharī* (Waves of Beauty):** a text in praise of the Goddess also attributed to Śaṅkara.

Upaniṣads: a body of texts which constitute the end section of the multilayered Vedas and hence also called Vedānta (*veda*+ *anta* [end]). Numerous texts claim the appellation. The so-called "classical Upaniṣads" are those on which famous Hindu traditional exegetes have commented. These include the two early "prose Upaniṣads" — the *Bṛhadāraṇyaka* (Great Forest Book) and the *Chāndogya* (Book of Psalm Reciters), and the later *Kauṣītaki-Brāhmaṇa Upaniṣad*, also in prose. Several other Upaniṣads such as the *Kena*, *Īśa*, *Maitrī*, *Muṇḍaka*, *Kaṭha*, *Taittirīya* and *Māṇḍūkya* are shorter in size and in verse, or prose and verse. The Upaniṣads are usually dated along a time-line stretching for *c.* 800 to 300 BCE.

***Devīmāhātmya* (Glorification of the Goddess):** A section of the *Mārkaṇḍeya Purāṇa*, devoted to the exaltation of the Goddess.

Vedārthasaṁgraha (Summation of the Meaning of the Vedas): A famous text by the eleventh century Hindu exegete Rāmānuja, which seeks to determine the purport of the Vedas.

Bhagavad-Gītā (Lord's Song): A section of the great epic, the *Mahābhārata*, which also functions as a text on its own. Usually assigned to second century BCE, it is perhaps the most widely used and accepted text within Hinduism.

Brahma Purāṇa (Ancient lore regarding Brahmā): The Purāṇas, eighteen in number, constitute a genre of sacred literature in Hinduism on their own, and detail the lives and adventures of gods and holy beings, including those of the three gods constituting the "Hindu trinity" — Brahmā, Viṣṇu and Śiva.

Manusmṛti (The Precepts of Manu): One of the best known representatives of the genre of Smṛti literature in Hinduism, when understood in the sense of "Law Books". It is usually assigned to the second century CE.

Ṛg-Veda (The Veda of Sacred Verses): The first and oldest of the "four" Vedas, which constitute the foundational scriptures of Hinduism. The *Ṛg-Veda* is usually assigned to *c.* 1500 BCE.

Advaita-Bodha-Dīpikā (The Lamp of Undual Enlightenment): A medieval digest of non-dualism, popular in the Advaitic circles.

Sarvadarśanasaṁgraha(Compendium of All Worldviews): A highly regarded survey of various schools of Indian philosophy prepared by Mādhavācārya, an Advaitin of the fourteenth century CE.

Śrimadbhāgavatam: Another name for the *Bhāgavata Purāṇa.*

Bhāgavata Purāṇa (Ancient Lore of the Lord): The most celebrated of the eighteen Purāṇas. It deals especially with the early life of Kṛṣṇa in loving detail, and is usually assigned to the ninth century CE.

Megasthênes: Author of a book on India (Indica) as it was in the fourth century BCE, now lost, excerpts of which are available in the writings of other scholars. He is believed to have been the Greek ambassador at the court of Candragupta Maurya.

Arrian: Author of an *Indica*, written around 150 BCE.

Albīrūnī: Author of a famous work on India, popularly known as *Alberuni's India*, who belongs to the eleventh century.

Arthaśāstra: (Treatise on Statecraft): A famous Hindu text on political and economic economy ascribed to Kauṭilya, whom tradition places in the fourth century BCE, and credits with master-minding the establishment of the Mauryan dynasty.

Kāmasūtra (Aphorisms of Passion): A manual on sex from classical India, composed by Vātsyāyana (*c.* CE 400-500)

Tiruvāymoḷi: A work of devotional poetry held on a par with the Veda in the Śrīvaiṣṇava tradition, revealed to Nammāḷvār, who lived between the eighth and the ninth century CE.

Śṛṅgāraśataka (Hundred Romantic Verses): One of the three compositions of 100 verses attributed to Bhartṛhari (seventh century CE). The other two deal with morality (*nīti*) and renunciation (*vairāgya*).

Brāhmaṇas (Priestly Pronouncements): One of the four divisions of the Vedas. Each of the four Vedas can be divided into four layers, respectively designated as the (1) Saṁhitā (verse collection); (2) Brāhmaṇa (priestly prose texts); (3) Āraṇyaka (forest-books); and (4) Upaniṣads (esoteric books). Passages have been cited from the *Aitareya Brāhmaṇa* and *Śatapatha Brāhmaṇa*, which belong respectively to the *Ṛg-Veda* and the *Yajur-Veda*.

Āraṇyakas: see Brāhmaṇas.

Mahābhārata: (The Account of the Epic Struggle Between the Members of the Bharata Lineage): Constitutes along with the *Rāmāyaṇa*, the great Itihāsas or epic narratives of classical India.

It is claimed to be "a hundred thousand verses" in length and is said to have assumed its present form over a period stretching from 400 BCE to CE 400.

Bibliography

Advaita Bodha Dīpikā [Lamp of Non-Dual Knowledge], Tiruvannamalai: Sri Ramanasramam, 1967.

Alston, A.J. (tr.), *The Method of the Vedanta: A Critical Account of the Advaita Tradition by Sri Swami Satchidanandendra Sarasvati*, London: Kegan Paul International, 1989.

Altekar, A.S., *The Position of Women in Hindu Civilization from Prehistorical Times to the Present Day*, Delhi: Motilal Banarsidass, 1973.

Apte, V.M., "Religion and Philosophy", in R.C. Majumdar (ed.), *The Vedic Age*, Bombay: Bharatiya Vidya Bhavan, 1965.

Bary, Wm. Theodore de, et al. (eds.), *Sources of Indian Tradition* (2nd edn.), New York: Columbia University Press, 1958.

Basham, A.L., *The Origins and Development of Classical Hinduism* (ed. Kenneth G. Zysk), Boston: Beacon Press, 1989.

———, *The Wonder That was India*, New Delhi: Rupa & Co., 1999 [1967].

Basu, Jogiraj, *India of the Age of the Brāhmaṇas*, Calcutta: Sanskrit Pustak Bhandar, 1969.

Bühler, G. (tr.), *The Laws of Manu*, Delhi: Motilal Banarsidass, 1964, first published 1886.

Buitenen, J.A.B. van (tr.), *The Mahābhārata*, Chicago and London: Chicago University Press, 1975, vol. II.

Chatterjee, Satischandra and Dhirendramohan Datta, *An Introduction to Indian Philosophy*, New Delhi: Rupa & Co., 2007.

Coburn, Thomas B., *Encountering the Goddess: A Translation of the Devīmahātmya and Study in Its Interpretation*, Albany, N.Y.: State University of New York Press, 1991.

Edgerton, Franklin, *The Bhagavad-Gītā*, Cambridge: Harvard University Press, 1974; first published 1944.

Eggeling, Julius (tr.), *The Śatapatha Brāhmaṇa*, Oxford: Clarendon Press, 1894.

Embree, Ainslie T. (ed.), *Alberuni's India*, New York: W.W. Norton & Company, 1971, part I.

Feuerstein, Georg, *The Bhagavad-Gītā: Yoga of Contemplation and Action*, New Delhi: Arnold-Heinemann [India] Pvt. Ltd., 1980.

Hiriyanna, M., *The Essentials of Indian Philosophy*, London: George Allen & Unwin, 1948.

Hospital, Clifford, *The Righteous Demon: A Study of Bali*, Vancouver: University of British Columbia, 1984.

Hume, Robert Ernest (tr.), *The Thirteen Principal Upanishads*, London: Oxford University Press, 1968; first published in England in 1921.

Joo, Swami Lakshman, *Kashmir Shaivism: The Secret Supreme* (ed. John Hughes), Albany, New York: State University of New York Press [The Universal Shaiva Trust], 1988.

Keith, Arthur Berriedale, *The Aitareya Āraṇyaka*, Oxford: Clarendon Press, 1909.

Klostermaier, Klaus K., *Hindu and Christian in Vrindaban*, London: SCM Press Ltd., 1969.

———, *A Survey of Hinduism*, Albany: State University of New York Press, 1988.

Kramrisch, Stella, *Manifestations of Shiva*, Philadelphia Museum of Art, 1981.

Law, Bimala Churn, *Concepts of Buddhism*, Leiden: Kern Institute, 1937.

Mahadevan, T.M.P., *Outlines of Hinduism*, Bombay: Chetana Ltd., 1971.

Majumdar, R.C. (ed.), *The Vedic Age*, Bombay: Bharatiya Vidya Bhavan, 1965 [1951].

Max Müller, F. (tr.), *The Dhammapada*, Oxford University Press, 1881; rpt. Motilal Banarsidass, 1973.

McCrindle, J.W., *Ancient India as Described by Megasthenês and Arrian* (revised 2nd edn. by R.C. Majumdar), Calcutta: Chuckervertty Chatterjee & Co., 1960.

Miller, Barbara Stoler, *The Bhagavadgītā: Kṛṣṇa's Counsel in Time of War*, New York: Columbia University Press, 1986.

——— (tr.), *Bhartrihari's Poems*, New York: Columbia University Press, 1967.

Narayan, Kirin, *Storytellers, Saints, and Scoundrels: Folk Narrative in Hindu Religious Teaching*, Delhi: Motilal Banarsidass, 1992.

Oldenberg, Hermann, *Vedic Hymns*, Oxford: Clarendon Press, 1897.

Pande, G.C., *Dimensions of Ancient Indian Social History*, New Delhi: Books & Books, 1984.

Prabhavananda, Swami and Christopher Isherwood, trs., *Crest Jewel of Discrimination*, Hollywood, California: Vedanta Press, 1947.

Radhakrishnan, S. (tr.), *The Brahma-Sūtra: The Philosophy of Spiritual Life*, New York: Harper & Brothers, 1960.

——— (ed.), *The Principal Upaniṣads*, London: George Allen & Unwin Ltd., 1953.

Radhakrishnan, Sarvepalli, and Charles A. Moore (eds.), *A Source Book of Indian Philosophy*, Princeton, New Jersey: Princeton University Press, 1957.

Raghavachar, S.S. (tr.), *Vedārtha-Saṁgraha of Śrī Rāmānujācārya*, Mysore: Sri Ramakrishna Mission, 1968.

Raghunathan, N. (tr.), *Śrīmadbhāgavatam*, Madras: Vighneswara Publishing House, 1976.

Renou, Louis (ed.), *Hinduism*, New York: George Braziller, 1962.

Renou, Louis, *The Nature of Hinduism* (tr. Patrick Evans), New York: Walker and Company, 1951.

Satchidananda Murty, K., *Revelation and Reason in Advaita Vedānta*, Waltair: Andhra University and New York: Columbia University, 1959.

Satchidananda Murty, K., *Vedic Hermeneutics*, Delhi: Motilal Banarsidass, 1993.

Sharvananda, Swami, "The Vedas and their Religious Teachings" in Haridas Bhattacharyya (ed.), *The Cultural Heritage of India*, Calcutta: The Ramakrishna Mission Institute of Culture, 1958, vol. I.

Smith, Huston, *The World's Religions*, San Francisco: Harper, 1991.

Soifer, Deborah A., *The Myths of Narasiṁha and Vāmana: Two Avatārs in Cosmological Perspective* Albany, N.Y.: State University of New York Press, 1991.

Spear, Percival (ed.), *The Oxford History of India* (4th edn.), Delhi: Oxford University Press, 1981.

Thibaut, George (tr.), *The Vedānta-Sūtras of Bādarāyaṇa with the Commentary of Śankara*, New York: Dover Publications, Inc., 1962: first published 1890 [Part I] and 1896 [Part II].

Zaehner, R.C. (tr.), *Hindu Scriptures*, New York: Dutton Everyman's Library, 1966.

Zimmer, Heinrich, *Myths and Symbols in Indian Art and Civilization* (ed. Joseph Campbell), New York and Evanston: Harper & Row, 1962.

Index